Word Processing

Word Processing Dictionary

Sylvia Dando

McGRAW-HILL BOOK COMPANY

London · New York · St Louis · San Francisco · Auckland · Bogotá
Guatemala · Hamburg · Lisbon · Madrid · Mexico · Montreal
New Delhi · Panama · Paris · San Juan · São Paulo · Singapore
Sydney · Tokyo · Toronto

Published by
McGRAW-HILL Book Company (UK) Limited
MAIDENHEAD · BERKSHIRE · ENGLAND

British Library Cataloguing in Publication Data

Dando, Sylvia
    Word processing dictionary.
    1. Word processing——Dictionaries
    I. Title
    652'.5'0321   Z52.25

ISBN 0-07-084993-5

Library of Congress Cataloging-in-Publication Data

Dando, Sylvia
    Word processing dictionary.

    1. Word processing--Dictionaries.   I. Title.
Z52.25.D36   1987   652'.5'0321   87-2610
ISBN 0-07-084993-5

2345 JWA 898

Typeset by J & K Hybert, Design & Type, Maidenhead.
Printed and bound in Great Britain by J.W. Arrowsmith Limited, Bristol.

abandon text   An operator may inadvertently make errors when text editing and wish to recall the document in its previous form. Many systems allow the operator to abandon editing and recall the previously stored version of the document.

abbreviation file   Often repeated words and phrases are keyed-in in abbreviated form but the whole word or phrase is inserted at the appropriate place in the text. The completed abbreviation file may be stored on disk and is available whenever required for a document assembly task.

The operator should keep a hard copy of the abbreviated identifiers in alphabetical order, together with their full meanings, for reference when a document is being prepared making use of the abbreviations facility.

Once the abbreviations file has been checked for accuracy, the operator can be sure that the spelling is correct each time the word(s) are merged with other text. This reduces proof reading time and is likely to be more accurate than keying in the text and using a spelling check function to confirm spellings.

abbreviation file (use of)   Once the abbreviation file has been prepared, the operator can recall the terms whenever they are required. The word processing system will usually require the operator to link a new document to the stored abbreviation file required, eg 'LEGALAB1' for a file containing specialist legal terminology. This is necessary so that the system can 'read' the coded abbreviations and their associated text when requested by the operator.

The abbreviation file facility is not available on all systems, but a suitable alternative procedure may be available, eg a number of short phrase memories, in which the specialist terms may be stored, may use each letter of the alphabet to store individual items. These phrase areas may or may not be lost when the system is switched off. If they are lost each time, it could still be worth while keying-in difficult spellings or phrases at the start of a long document in order to save time.

abort   The termination of a routine or program, usually when a fault of some kind occurs.

accents Accented characters used in foreign languages, eg å ø ç é, can usually be obtained by pressing a combination of keys.

access The process of *writing to* or *reading from* information/data in the system's memory.

access time The time taken to *read data from* or *write data to* a memory device. ·

acoustic coupler A modem which permits the transmission of data over the telephone lines from one computer system to another by converting the computer's digital signals to the analog signals used by the telephone system – the process is then reversed by the receiving modem. The identifying feature is a special cradle which is shaped to accept a normal telephone handset, allowing the computer system direct access to the telephone network. This is a temporary connection and the telephone line is available for normal use as soon as the data has been transmitted.

acoustic hood A printer cover or hood to reduce noise generated during printing – high speed daisywheel printers are particularly noisy.

algorithm The sequence of steps required to provide the solution to a problem.

alignment New text is aligned vertically and horizontally with existing text.

alphanumeric A description of information, or a keyboard, using alphabetic and numeric characters.

anti-static Static electricity in the atmosphere can be reduced by using an anti-static spray or mat.

anti-static cleaner An anti-static cleaning fluid is used for cleaning and to reduce static electricity. Wiping over the screen and the casing of the equipment helps to reduce the amount of dust attracted to the terminal.

append   Adding new information at the end of an existing document/file.

applications program   A computer program designed for a specific purpose, eg payroll.

archival storage   Information kept for infrequent reference and as a back-up to current files.

arithmetic/logic unit   Part of the central processing unit which performs arithmetic, eg addition and multiplication, and non-arithmetic (logic) tasks, eg sorting records.

artificial intelligence   Systems which can modify and improve their operations by reasoning and by learning from the results of their actions.

ascender   Part of a lower case letter which extends above the main part of the character, eg b d h.

ASCII   (pronounced Askee) **A**merican **S**tandard **C**ode for **I**nformation **I**nterchange. A computer code which represents characters within a system. It has been adopted by manufacturers of various makes of equipment and enables a degree of compatibility.

author   The person who prepares text, by dictation or manuscript, for processing.

automatic page numbering   The operator states on which page the numbering should commence and what the first number should be – no revision is necessary by the operator after editing or reformatting.

automatic pagination   The system divides a multi-page document into pages of a specified length defined by the operator, eg 58 lines.

automatic paragraph numbering   Although it is easy for an operator to number paragraphs as text is keyed-in, it is sometimes necessary to re-number after text editing has taken place. By inserting a code, instead of a number, some systems will automatically renumber the paragraphs if the sequence is changed by movement or insertion of additional paragraphs. The screen may display the number or the code, depending on the system being used.

automatic repeat   A key which is pressed on the keyboard will repeat until released.

background memory   Tasks undertaken by the system direct, without the operator's attention. The operator works in the foreground and the system takes care of the background.

background printing   A facility which allows the operator to proceed with other tasks while printing takes place, eg a mail merge while keying-in or editing another document.

backing storage   Disk storage which can be linked to the main memory of the computer and is therefore not lost when the system is turned off.

backlog   Work which has been prepared for processing but which the operator has not yet commenced.

backspace   A key which moves the cursor one character to the left each time it is pressed.

back-up   In addition to the disk being used there should be at least one additional copy (back-up) that can be used in the event of disk failure or other problem.

bandwidth   Measures the amount of information that can flow through a cable in a telecommunications channel.

bar and code scanning devices   A light pen or wand reader can be used to record information electronically, eg in libraries, retail and wholesale stores, and as an aid to stock control.

BASIC   Beginners' All-purpose Symbolic Instruction Code. A computer programming language which is widely used on a variety of computers.

batch   Work of a similar kind which could be processed in one batch or operation.

baud rate   Measurement of the bits per second travelling from one part of a computer to another or to a different system.

benchmark   Selected material used to test flexibility of system performance and give comparative information about different systems.

bi-directional   Lines of text are printed alternately left to right and right to left, thus increasing the speed of printing.

binary   A means of counting used by computers consisting of only two values 0 or 1 – 'on' or 'off'.

bit   A binary digit, ie 0 or 1, with eight bits equalling one byte.

bits   A description of the number of pieces of information a computer can process at one time, eg a 16 bit computer transmits 16 bits/pieces of information at one time.

bits per second (bps)   Measure for describing the transfer rate of a communication channel.

block   A portion of text which is defined by the operator and treated as one unit by the system.

boilerplate   Combining blocks of pre-recorded standard text with customised details to produce a personalised document.

The operator begins by creating a separate document and indicates to the system the standard paragraph file required. The operator may combine text keyed-in directly from the keyboard with the stored text. It may be necessary for the standard text and the separate document to have the same format, ie identical rulers, pitch etc.

The operator presses the appropriate command key(s), enters the coded identifier then presses the ENTER key. The system will automatically select the standard paragraph file and insert the text into the new document at the position of the cursor. The standard paragraph file is not displayed on the screen.

bold   Text is printed with each character darker and slightly wider than usual. It is an ideal means of emphasizing text.

boot   To start up the system using the system or program disk.

bottom margin   The space between the end of a piece of text and the end of the sheet of paper.

bubble memory   Compact, reliable and permanent way of storing large volumes of computer information on magnetic *bubbles* in a thin film of material. It is more robust than the floppy disk but is expensive in comparison. Instead of moving past a read/write head, these bubbles are pushed through a layer of magnetic material, which provides a high volume memory with no moving parts.

buffer memory   Stores text temporarily while the operator decides on the next operation, eg moving a piece of text to a new location, or linking operations between a number of input and output devices.

bug   An error in the program which prevents it from performing correctly.

bureau   An organisation providing hardware and expertise in computing and/or word processing for anyone without such facilities, or for anyone requiring short-term additional facilities.

bus/data bus   Data travels between the memory and the processor along a data bus. The number of tracks (wires) on the data bus, eg 16, indicates the number of bits/pieces of information that can be dealt with at one time.

byte   Eight bits. The smallest unit of information handled by the computer. One byte is used to represent a single character, eg a letter, number or punctuation mark.

calculation and verification   Some systems have a maths program which provides facilities for calculation of both horizontal and vertical columns. An additional numeric keypad may also be incorporated on the right-hand side of the keyboard.

calculator   A built-in calculator enables simple arithmetic tasks to be undertaken within word processing tasks.

capitalisation   On some systems it is possible to change text from upper case to lower case and vice versa without re-keying the text.

carbon ribbon A thin plastic-coated ribbon giving high quality appearance but generally only used once, and therefore expensive. Ideal for external correspondence but a fabric ribbon should be used for draft and internal documents.

care of disks
DO keep flexible magnetic disks in their wallets because they are anti-static and prevent contamination by dust.
DO write on the label before sticking it on the disk.
DO make sure every disk is labelled correctly.
DO store disks in a vertical position in a suitable box.
DO keep an index of all disks and files.
DO keep a hard copy of stored text.

DO NOT bend, fold or otherwise manipulate disks.
DO NOT touch any of the exposed areas of the disk as this can cause corruption.
DO NOT put disks on top of the VDU, printer, power cables, telephones or other sources of magnetism.
DO NOT force a disk into a drive or into its wallet.
DO NOT stack disks in a horizontal pile.
DO NOT leave disks lying in the sun or near heaters or fridges.
DO NOT eat, drink or smoke near the disks.

care of the word processor
DO follow manufacturer's cleaning recommendations.
DO use a dust cover when equipment is not in use.
DO disconnect from power supply before moving equipment.
DO have a servicing contract.

DO NOT eat or drink near the equipment.
DO NOT smoke near the equipment.
DO NOT attempt to mend the equipment if a breakdown occurs.

carriage return A description inherited from typewriters, now usually referred to simply as *return*, whereby the cursor returns to the left-hand margin when the RETURN key is pressed.

cartridge disk A large round high-capacity disk housed in a plastic cartridge.

cartridge ribbon A printer ribbon contained within a cartridge which enables replacements to be made quickly and easily.

cat A ball embedded in the surface of the workstation near the keyboard which can be moved easily with the fingertips to direct the cursor on the screen.

cathode ray tube (CRT) Similar to a television screen which displays text as it is entered via the keyboard or recalled from storage. Incorporated in the VDU.

central processing unit (CPU) Used to control and co-ordinate the various functions of the system, as directed by the software program. The microprocessor controls the 'brain' of the computer system linking together all the components and manipulating data. It is responsible for:
– accepting text from the keyboard and storing it in memory
– displaying text on the screen
– accepting commands from the operator and carrying them out
– arranging the text to be printed
– controlling the operation of the printer and disks.

centre tab Text is centred equally on either side of the tab point.

centring Words, lines, paragraphs or whole pages may be centred between left and right margins by inserting appropriate instruction, without any calculations by the operator.

character A single letter, number, symbol or punctuation mark which can be displayed on the screen or printed.

character formation Characters on the screen are made up of tiny dots of light, known as pixels, although this is not always apparent to the human eye. The rows and columns of dots form a grid, called a matrix. This also applies when a dot matrix printer is used, but daisywheel printers produce fully formed characters.

character printer Individual characters printed consecutively on the paper by an impact printer, ie the same method as a typewriter.

character set The total number of characters which can be displayed on a VDU.

character string   Any group of alphabetic/numeric/additional characters.

characters per inch (cpi)   A measurement of printing pitch, eg 12 cpi.

characters per second (cps)   A measurement of printing speed, eg 22 cps.

charge-back costing system   The cost of word processing must be allocated to individuals or departments within the company, so that departmental budgets for word processing can be realistically prepared according to actual usage. This ensures that departments not using word processing facilities do not subsidise others.

check space on disk   Before keying-in a new document it is always advisable to check the remaining space on the disk, to ensure that the document can be stored after keying-in. When a disk is almost full, it is advisable to check that all the documents are still required as deletion will release space for new documents.

chip   Intricate circuitry built up layer by layer on a small rectangular piece of very thin silicon.

choosing a word processor   The variety of systems available can be very confusing to inexperienced managers and operators. Before purchasing any system it is advisable not only to see a demonstration of the equipment, but also to visit firms currently using the same system for the same type of work, to establish advantages and disadvantages. Another useful exercise is to present the supplier with some of the proposed work to be undertaken by the system and see how easy it is for this to be done.

cleaning kits   Special recommended cleaning kits are available for disk drive heads, hard disks, printers and screens. Nothing else should ever be used.

cluster   More than one workstation sharing common storage, eg Winchester disk, and/or printing facilities.

column   Horizontal space used by a single character on a VDU.

column manipulation   Tabulated columns may be moved to change the sequence, to create new columns or to merge columns.

command sequence   A series of operating instructions for a specific task.

communicating word processors   Word processors are excellent for providing letter-quality transmission of electronic mail at high speeds – an A4 page of text may take less than 15 seconds.

If the word processors are not compatible, it is necessary to be linked to a local area network for local transmissions or to the public telex or teletex networks to provide national or international telecommunications. This enables them to take advantage of message switching and store and forward systems.

communication packages   Packages providing the capability for direct communication between terminals using a modem. Access to public databases, eg Prestel, or databanks may also be possible.

communications   Text (mail) can be transferred electronically between computers and/or word processors in a different location via a communications network. Word processing communications equipment comprises hardware (modem) and software. The hardware contains all the electronics for the interface, speed and timing control. The software provides 'fine tuning' for a specific make of equipment.

Internal mail may be keyed-in by the operator, approved by the author and sent electronically to its destination(s) which may be within the same building, in different parts of the country or overseas. At the receiving workstation, the screen would show a list of all the electronic mail waiting to be viewed. 'Mail' can be viewed on the screen, or printed out if a hard copy is required. If the individual has a workstation, then a reply may be keyed-in immediately and despatched in the same way to the originator without the need to commit the memo to paper.

compact floppy disk   The floppy disk is contained within a rigid plastic case. The 3″ and 3½″ disks are most likely to be supplied in this type of casing.

compatible   Two computers are said to be compatible if a program written on one will run on the other without modification.

computer   A general name for a system which is capable of computing and/or word processing applications.

computer assisted retrieval (CAR)   A very quick means of retrieving information recorded on microfilm. Special codes are entered into the computer by the operator as each document is photographed and these are recorded automatically on the microfilm. Documents may be indexed by several features, eg date or reference, providing a variety of methods of searching. The computer can search for the codes and retrieve the requested information rapidly – the sequence of the documents is irrelevant and they can therefore be stored in random sequence.

The microfilm may be viewed using a special display/reader device, and it may also have an option available to produce a printed copy.

computer-based message systems (CBMS)   Communication via electronic mail of keyboarded text using electronic mailbox facilities.

computer literacy   An awareness of computers including how they work and what they do.

computer mailbox service   A computer mailbox service is an electronic mailing system which operates on a *store and retrieve* basis, rather than on a *store and forward* basis. After despatch the message is stored until the recipient chooses to read it. If the system is linked to radio-paging facilities the recipient is alerted if a message is still waiting to be read after a specified period of time. The computer mailbox service may be provided within a company network or rented from a public-access network.

computer output microfilm (COM)   A photographic process of printing computer output as reels of microfilm or on microfiche instead of paper. Large quantities of information can be stored in a very small space by this means.

COM is used for information required mainly for reference, eg technical manuals, spare parts catalogues. It is also useful for storing information which must be retained for security or legal reasons as it can be stored using the minimum amount of space.

configuration   Components which make up a total word processing system (central processing unit, VDU, keyboard, printer and disk drive). eg a stand-alone system.

consumable supplies   Adequate supplies of disks, ribbons, daisywheels and paper must always be in stock, and stock records must be accurately maintained.

continuous stationery   A continuous ream of paper is folded into a pile which can be opened up like a fan. The paper is perforated at each fold, allowing single sheets to be torn off. The paper may be standard computer printout paper or pre-printed invoices, letterheads, payslips, etc. On the left and right sides of the paper there are detachable strips punched with sprocket holes for use on a tractor-feed device on the printer. When the strips are removed the paper has a reasonably smooth edge.

control/function keys   Usually referred to as dedicated function keys. Used specifically for editing and other functions, eg insert, delete, merge, format, store page, tabs. A set of four or five arrow keys may also be available specifically for movement of the cursor.

copy   Text is defined and copied to an additional location without being deleted from its original position.

copy a disk   Disk copying is a very important housekeeping function which applies to both system and working disks. The identification label should be completed immediately the copy is made.

It is essential for at least one copy of the system disk to be made on another disk – preferably two – in case of failure of the original. The copy should be stored in a different location from the original to avoid a complete loss, eg in case of fire or theft.

It is essential to copy a working disk containing documents to be edited or re-used, which probably means the majority of working disks. The duplicate disk is known as a back-up disk, a security copy, or an archive disk.

Care must be taken to ensure that the copying procedure is carried out in the right direction, ie from the *copy from* disk to the *copy to* disk. If the procedure is carried out in reverse the blank or previously used disk will be over-written on to the 'master' disk and all the latter's contents will be lost, ie the original is lost and there is no copy!

copy a document from one disk to another   After a security/back-up copy of a working disk has been made, it is essential to keep it up to date. At the end of each day any documents created, or existing documents edited or altered in any way, must be copied on to the back-up disk. It may be necessary to copy one document at a time or several selected documents in one operation. This selective back-up saves making a complete new copy of the disk, but it may be quicker to actually recopy the disk.

In addition to updating back-up disks the operator may need to copy a single document from one disk to another. For example:

- When a disk is almost full and text is to be edited or added to a document, it is advisable to copy the document to an alternative disk to ensure there is adequate space for the amendments.

- A number of operators may prepare part of a very long document to enable the work to be carried out quickly. When each operator has keyed-in their section, the complete document is assembled on one disk.

- A standard paragraph file is prepared and copied so that each operator has an identical copy.

copy block/cut and leave   A defined piece of text is stored within the temporary memory and used elsewhere in a document, but also remains in its original position.

copyholder   A free-standing copyholder or one attached to the side of the VDU is preferred by some operators to having papers flat on the desk when copying or editing text. Most have a line guide or ruler which is moved down the page as work progresses.

copyright   Copyright for software disks containing word processing programs denies the purchaser the right to make multiple copies of the disks without permission. Purchasers may make one or two copies of the disks for their own security purposes.

correction of draft text   To avoid confusion, text authors should use standard correction signs and make all changes in red ink. NEVER delete with correction fluid or cut the pages and paste into a new position. A few examples are given on page 14:

14   CORRESPONDENCE QUALITY

MARGIN SIGN	SIGN IN TEXT	MEANING
del ♂	/	Delete text crossed out
a𝇋 ;𝇋	𝇋	Insert character, word, punctuation as indicated
uc or CAPS	—	Text underlined to be in capitals
lc	⟋	Text underlined to be in lower case
NP or //	[or //	Start new paragraph
run on	⌒⌒⟋	Do not start a new paragraph
stet	………	Leave word with dots/dashes underneath as it was
⌒	⌒	No space required
#	𝇋	Insert a space
trs	2⌣1⌣3	Transpose (change the order of) as indicated

correspondence quality   An alternative description for letter-quality printing, usually required for external documents.

corrupt   Destruction of recorded text by the system or by operator malfunction.

CP/M   **C**ontrol **P**rogram for **M**icroprocessors. A standard operating system stored in the internal memory and used on many different computer systems. A word processing program will take over from the CP/M until the operator terminates the word processing program when the CP/M resumes control. Disk management and other housekeeping routines, eg copying disks, may use the CP/M.

crash   A computer program which is running but cannot be completed or restarted, ie a breakdown.

cursor   The cursor occupies one character space and indicates to the operator where text is to be entered, revision made or the position for an instruction to commence or finish. The cursor can take several forms – stationary or flashing, solid rectangle or underline.

cursor control keys   The cursor can be moved to any position on the screen, in any direction – vertical, horizontal or diagonal. Most systems have clearly marked cursor control keys, eg ↑ ↓ ← →. Movement by character or line may be increased to word, paragraph or page by using an additional key.

cut and leave/copy block   A defined piece of text is stored within the temporary memory and used elsewhere in a document, but also remains in its original position.

cut and paste   A piece of text is defined and moved from its original position to another.

daisywheel   A circular typing element, with a character at the end of each *petal*, which is easily changed when a different typeface is required.

daisywheel printer   The daisywheel rotates until the required character is in position for a hammer to fly out and hit it, transferring the character through a ribbon on to paper. This is probably the most common type of impact printer used for word processing as the high quality print makes it ideal for external use.

data   Information (data) in the form of numbers or characters which the computer program understands.

data bank   A database which is accessed via different terminals by many people.

database   A collection of files of information to which the computer has access, eg clients' names and addresses, personnel records.

data bus   Data travels between the memory and the processor along a data bus. The number of tracks (wires) on the data bus, eg 16, indicate the number of bits/pieces of information that can be dealt with at one time.

Data Protection Act 1984   This Act affects all users of computer-based equipment. Any personal data stored must be registered, together with reasons for requiring and disclosing the data. There are a few exemptions to registration but it is important to note that not only employers, but anyone using a computer for recording data, eg for a charity/club is likely to be liable for registration. The general principles state that the data must be:

- correct and kept up to date
- erased when no longer necessary
- only disclosed to registered recipients
- only stored for lawful registered purposes

and that:

- precautions must be taken to prevent unauthorised access and use
- opportunity must be given for a data subject to object to personal data being recorded
- anyone mentioned in the data has the right to see it and to take legal action seeking compensation if information is, for example, inaccurate, or disclosed to unauthorised sources.

The following terms used in the Act should be noted:

- *Data* is information stored in a form which permits electronic processing.
- *Personal data* is information enabling an individual to be identified.
- *Data subject* is an individual who is the subject of personal data.
- *Data user* is an individual who 'holds' data.
- *Computer bureau* refers to an individual either allowing access under supervision to recorded data or processing data as an agent for others.

Full details of the Act are available from the Data Protection Registrar, Springfield House, Water Lane, Wilmslow, Cheshire, SK9 5AX. Registration packs are available from any Crown Post Office or the Registrar's Office.

de-bug   To search for, isolate and correct errors in a system or program.

decimal tab   An additional tab facility providing automatic alignment of columns of figures. The tab needs to be set at the position for the decimal point. The decimal tab may be a special code which is used with the normal tab key, or it may be an ordinary tab used with a decimal tab key. A tab key is used to move to the column and the system enters the figures left to right (backwards) until the decimal point is entered and the remaining figures then appear right to left (normal).

dedicated function keys   Keys with specific functions to assist the operator, eg DELETE   INSERT   CUT   PASTE   FIND.

dedicated word processor   Designed only for word processing and generally capable of:

- editing text on screen by inserting and deleting
- moving words, sentences, paragraphs and columns
- automatic numbering of pages
- justifying margins
- automatic decimal alignment
- scrolling text vertically and horizontally on the screen
- displaying 'prompts' to guide the operator
- merging documents
- printing from background memory.

Refinements include:

- revealing the bottom line of a preceding page and the top line of the following page on the screen at the same time
- checking the spelling of words against a built-in 'dictionary'
- transmitting documents direct from one word processor to another using electronic mail facilities.

Advantages

- All the system's internal and external features are designed and built with only word processing in mind.

- The keyboard only has the keys that are needed. Each major function has its own key, with a unique label which may be coloured or have a symbol for easier use.

- Some keyboards are detached from the screen so the operator can position according to individual preference.

- The screen display is often better than on a computer, and tilting and swivelling give better positioning.

- Hardware design takes word processing into account in terms of available memory, communications, options, size, type and number of characters on the screen.

- The software takes full advantage of the hardware. It is fast, and of good quality, because it was designed for use by non-computer users.

- All the above features generally mean that a dedicated word processor is easier to use than a computer-based system and may be referred to as *user friendly*.

Disadvantages

- Dedicated word processors are very expensive.

- A dedicated word processor restricts the variety of tasks which may be undertaken.

- If computer capabilities are required a further system will have to be purchased.

- Most manufacturers offer means of expanding or upgrading their systems but this is within a certain framework – limited to their disks, printers, etc.

- What is gained in having a powerful easy-to-use word processor, is lost in flexibility.

defaults   A set of pre-stored settings relating to document layout, eg margins, page length, tabs, pitch. Used in all new documents unless the operator makes any necessary changes.

deletion   Characters, words, lines or paragraphs of text may be deleted at any point within a document. It is advisable to reformat after deleting items to ensure that wraparound has occurred throughout the text.

deletion of documents/files   When the operator is absolutely certain that text is no longer required it can be deleted from the disk. Some systems allow automatic deletion of documents after a specified period of time.

descender   That part of a lower case letter which appears below the main part of the character, eg g j p q y.

deskilling   Introduction of new technology may mean that old skills are no longer required but new skills will be needed. Employees who are adaptable and willing to learn new skills will continue to be employed.

device   Parts of the hardware referred to as a device are the printer, screen and disk drive. An error code or the words 'device not ready' indicates to the operator, for example, that the printer is awaiting paper.

diagnostic   Usually refers to a disk which the engineer will use to establish faults.

dictionary   A list of words stored on disk enabling a spelling check to be undertaken by the system.

difference between a dedicated word processor and a microcomputer with word processing software

- A dedicated word processor is a very expensive item but it may have specific function keys for each main task which make it easier for an operator to use.

- A computer system using mnemonics may have a simpler keyboard but the operator is required to learn many codes.

- Where a suitable microcomputer is already in use for data processing, or where flexibility is needed, a word processing package will normally be available as an 'add-on' feature.

- A word processing software package, eg Wordstar or NewWord, is distributed on a disk and must be *read* into the system. With the addition of a good quality printer a very acceptable economic word processing system is the result.

direct access   The system finds information by moving directly to the appropriate track on the disk, rather than scanning through the whole disk.

direct printing   The operator is able to key-in and print without the necessity to store the text in the memory or on disk. Some systems print simultaneously, as on a typewriter, but others only print after the RETURN key is pressed.

directory/index   Lists documents recorded on storage medium and indicates disk capacity used and/or still available.

discretionary/soft hyphen   A hyphen may be inserted to divide a word at a line-end to improve the appearance of the text. If the line length is altered the hyphen will disappear if no longer appropriate.

disk/diskette   A flat magnetic disk on which data and text are stored. It may be used to store the word processing software which has to be loaded into the system and/or to store text long-term after it has been created. Information is read by random access – any part of a disk is accessed very quickly.

disk drives   Disk drives contain read/write heads to record and retrieve information stored on disk. May be incorporated in the casing of the VDU or may be a completely separate unit connected by a cable. Single disk drives only accommodate one disk in the system at a time and this may be a problem if disks need to be copied regularly. Dual or twin disk drives can accommodate two disks, eg the program disk and the working disk, and copying is undertaken quickly and easily.

disk index/directory/catalogue   The operator is able to obtain information about documents stored on a particular disk, eg

- name or reference of document
- size of document, amount of disk space used
- space remaining for storage
- date on which document created
- date of revision.

disk operating system (DOS)   The operating system is stored on disk.

disk sizes The most commonly used disk sizes are 8″, 5¼″ and 3½″ depending on the size of the disk drive being used. The storage capacity of these disks varies from system to system. The disk directory can be used to verify remaining capacity at any time.

disk space remaining The system will indicate to the operator the disk space used and that remaining unused. The format of this information will vary with individual systems.

display format The total number of characters, or lines and characters per line, which may be displayed on the VDU.

document/file Text stored on disk as one unit may be called a document or file – the term used varies between systems. Each document/file must be named for easy recall.

document assembly Documents compiled using standard stored text with variable information added. Very useful where standard paragraphs of text are frequently used to compile wills, conveyances, etc.

document based systems The operator does not need to observe page endings as the page breaks are inserted automatically, depending on the number of lines stipulated in the format instructions. Movement of text from one page to another is extremely easy, with page adjustments automatically taking place. Precautions must be taken to ensure the page break does not occur in an inappropriate position.

document names The system may restrict the number of characters in the name of a file/document to 8 characters, with an option of a further 3 after a full stop, eg DOCUMENT.010. A file/document may be re-named whenever necessary. Names can be displayed in alphabetical, numerical or date order on screen or paper.

document recovery Some systems provide a facility to enable a document which has been accidentally deleted to be recovered from memory.

dot matrix printer Dot matrix printers build a character as a matrix or array of dots using a series of electrically hammered fine pins – quality depends on the number of pins in the matrix which varies, eg

5 × 7 or 9 × 24; the more the better. Draft printing quality is not as good as other impact printers but it is generally much faster. To produce near letter-quality print the speed may be reduced and/or each line is printed twice (multi-pass) allowing more dots to fill the gaps left on the first printout. A big advantage is the provision to vary the shape and size of the characters and the printing of graphics.

double density disks   Text is stored very densely within each sector on the disk, approximately twice the number of characters per disk track as on single density disks.

double-head disk drive   This type of disk drive is necessary when double sided disks are used to permit access to either side of the disk.

double sided disks   Disks which store text on both sides and require a double-head disk drive which can access from either side of the disk without the operator removing the disk from the drive.

down time   Time when equipment is not in use due to breakdown or malfunction.

draft copy   A document which may need editing is printed, probably in double spacing, for the text author to amend and return to the operator. After editing only the altered sections need be checked.

dumb terminal   A terminal without any processing capability of its own. It therefore relies entirely on the central processing unit to which it must be linked at all times.

duplex   A telecommunication link enabling transmission to take place in both directions at the same time.

duplication of documents/files   For security 'back-up' it is essential that all documents/files should be copied at least daily, but the expense of duplicate disks sometimes makes a firm reluctant to do this. However, only one disaster is necessary to make them realise that back-up disks are much cheaper than having to redo days, weeks or even months of work which has been lost.

edit   Text may need correcting (editing) because either the operator has made mistakes or the text author has had a change of mind. Characters, words, lines or paragraphs may be inserted or deleted at any point within a document.

electronic communication   It is unnecessary for an operator or user to understand the technical intricacies of how electronic communication systems actually work. The operator needs to be aware of the equipment available in the office, the facilities, the level of performance and how to operate and control it. Manufacturers are increasingly aware that this type of equipment must be simple to operate, and the user is generally helped by menus from which selections can be made with the help of prompts from the system.

electronic diary   Software is available to enable diaries to be maintained on a computer allowing details of appointments to be keyed-in, sorted and viewed on the VDU. When a meeting has to be arranged between several employees the system is able to search the diaries for a suitable time, without the need to contact the individuals personally.

electronic filing   Filing and retrieval of documents and/or information using software and electronic devices. As with manual filing, the system must be easy to operate and kept up-to-date.

electronic mail   Text and/or graphics can be transmitted as digital information direct from one workstation to another at high speed by two-way telecommunication. The 'mail' is displayed visually and, in contrast to the post, need not be in hard copy form. Electronic mail may also provide additional functions whereby a document could automatically be sent to everyone on a distribution list.

Electronic mail attempts to cut down on the volume of paper that is processed using a quicker, easier method which is less prone to error and generally neater than conventional paperwork. The main difficulty encountered is non-compatibility of equipment within and between organisations.

electronic mailbox   Each person linked to the system has their own *mail box* or *pigeon hole* which receives messages sent by other users. By periodically *opening* the mail box the messages are received. Work is not interrupted when a message arrives and the operator does not have to be there to receive it. Information received may be stored in the mailbox until it is displayed on screen, and only printed if a hard copy is necessary, or it can be deleted or redirected as appropriate.

electronic message   There are two parts to an electronic message, representing the envelope and the text (letter/memo) used in the manual method. The 'envelope' contains the addressee details and the 'message' indicates the subject, time sent, etc, followed by the actual message content.

electronic message system   A message system would include facilities such as in tray, pending tray, notes, reminder file, diary, message editing, word processing, calculator, waste bin, records.

electronic office   A general term referring to an office using computer-based systems. An automated electronic office should include text creation and editing facilities, electronic mail for receiving and despatching messages, electronic filing for storing and retrieving information, and possibly teleconferencing.

electronic typewriters   There are three main components to an electronic typewriter

- the keyboard with typing keys and function keys
- the memory unit with limited storage capacity, from a few characters to a few pages
- a printing unit with a daisywheel printing element.

Simple editing facilities include self-correcting, stop codes, paragraph indents, text insertion/deletion/movement, search and replace, 15-35 character display, built-in memory. Short pieces of standard text which are used regularly, eg date, reference, complimentary close, can be stored and recalled when required.

Automatic typing functions include carrier return, underscoring, centring, tabulation, decimal tab and relocation.

Automatic printing functions include paper feed, justifying, emboldening, page numbering, headers and footers. However, an electronic typewriter cannot print out a document or letter and at the same time allow the operator to be editing or keying-in new text.

More advanced electronic typewriters may also have a VDU which displays a single or part line (thin window display) of text and a storage unit which uses a mini-flexible diskette. With additional memory facilities the equipment can undertake many word processing tasks.

élite   The name given to a horizontal printing pitch which produces 12 characters per inch.

emboldening   Text produced in a much darker print by using multi-strike and/or shadow printing techniques. Text to be emboldened must be defined by the operator but the effect does not usually appear on the screen as it is a printing command.

emulation   One computer system imitates another to enable communication between the two systems to take place.

encryption   Communication channels as well as computers and disks must be protected against loss or access by unauthorised persons when data is being stored or transmitted. *Data encryption* or cryptography may be better known as scrambling and is simply a means of ensuring security throughout a communications network.

Information is protected from disclosure by converting it into cyphertext so that it is unintelligible to anyone without the key. This process helps to protect against accidental disclosures, wire-tapping and other electronic forms of 'snooping' by a hacker. Cypher or code keys may be changed as often as wished, eg monthly, weekly, daily or even more often.

No code or cypher is perfect but the aim of security measures of this type is to make the cost of breaking the code greater than the value of the information protected.

epilepsy   VDUs may flicker at a rate that brings on fits in epileptics; adjustment of the controls can usually remove the flicker.

erase   If the space bar is used to erase text a gap will remain even after reformatting, unlike deletion, when text is completely reformatted.

ergonomics The analysis of the relationship between an operator, the workstation, the environment and the physical and psychological needs arising from the working situation. Manufacturers and employers are becoming more aware of the need to consider ergonomic factors when designing or selecting equipment. Well-designed equipment can reduce operator fatigue and discomfort and increase productivity.

error detection A feature which can be incorporated in a communications system to ensure that text has not been distorted during transmission.

error message A code, or message, which appears if a machine fault occurs or an incorrect or incomplete command is given which the word processor is unable to recognise and execute.

execute Pressing the execute (EXEC) key enables the operator to verify a command before it is implemented.

execution time The time taken to complete (execute) commands given to the system.

exit Departure from one routine to another, eg editing to printing.

external memory A permanent or long-term memory, eg a disk, for software programs or text.

external storage Any storage medium, eg disk, which can be removed from the system and stored elsewhere.

eyes Screen glare should be reduced as much as possible by adjusting screen angle, brightness and contrast. Careful choice of screen colours with non-flicker screen image and of room lighting and non-reflective decor will help to provide an environment which is restful to the eyes – adequate lighting of a suitable type should be provided. Regular eye tests are essential for operators already wearing glasses or contact lenses as well as those with 'good' eyesight.

fabric ribbon An inexpensive ribbon made of nylon or cotton. Very economical to use because it rotates many times before the ink fades and a replacement has to be fitted to the printer. Ideal for internal and draft documents.

facsimile (FAX)   A scanning device that transmits over the telephone lines a copy of a document one page at a time, for reproduction at the point of destination. An A4 page can take less than a minute to be transmitted. Modern machines have facilities to enable automatic transmission to multiple addresses, store and forward facilities for automatic overnight transmission (at cheaper rates) and unattended receipt. The machine can receive transmitted documents, cut the paper to length and stack it, without the need for an operator to be in attendance.

An important advantage over other electronic mail systems is that it requires little or no change in work methods. Mail is still written, typed and filed and because facsimile systems scan the whole page, they can be used to send non-textual information – such as illustrations, maps, graphs, etc – which would be difficult or impossible to transmit using other systems.

fanfold   A continuous ream of paper is folded into a pile which can be opened up like a fan. The paper is perforated at each fold so that single sheets can be torn off. The paper may be standard computer printout paper or pre-printed invoices, letterheads, payslips, etc. On the left and right sides of the paper there are detachable strips punched with sprocket holes for use on a tractor-feed device on the printer. When the strips are removed the paper has a reasonably smooth edge.

feasibility study   An investigation to establish the need or otherwise of, for example, purchasing word processing equipment. The points to consider would be:

- company's routine work and any specific requirements
- volume of paperwork currently produced
- present system of preparing paperwork
- advantages and disadvantages of current system
- volume of work to be transferred to new system
- staff reaction
- installation and running costs
- local suppliers – training, maintenance.

fields A sorting category used when processing a records file, eg name, address, telephone number. In the example below the first column contains the field names and the second, field values. The complete block forms a record which would be stored with an identifier (at the beginning) and a terminator (at the end) to indicate the length of the record. Each record within a specific records file would contain identical field names.

FNA   Mary Anne
SNA   Jones
NME   Miss M A Jones
SAL   Miss Jones
DOB   24 12 1960
STR   14 Chestnut Avenue
TOW   Bath
COU   Avon
PCD   BA4 3JL
TEL   0276 654321
MST   Single

file/document Text stored on disk as one unit may be called a file or a document – the term used varies between systems. Each file/document must be named for easy recall.

firmware Program contained within the *read only memory* chip in the hardware.

fixed disk A fixed disk cannot be removed from the disk drive as it is a built-in unit, eg Winchester disk.

flag characters These may appear on the screen to indicate to the operator a hard return, unused lines at end of the document, overprinting line with the next, etc.

floppy disk/flexible disk Magnetic recording medium made of flexible plastic contained in a square rigid envelope for protection. The disk should also be kept in a dust jacket for further protection. Apertures in the protective cover permit data on the disk to be accessed quickly by the read/write heads in the disk drive.

font Type face and size a printer can produce from one print source, eg a daisywheel.

footer   A short piece of information which is printed automatically within the bottom margin of each page or selected pages of a multi-page document, eg a reference. The operator determines the depth of the bottom margin and may instruct for odd and even pages to be printed in a different horizontal position if unequal margins are being used.

footnote   A reference symbol within the main body of text is also entered at the bottom of the page with a detailed explanation or reference.

foreground memory   Used when the operator is keying-in and editing text.

foreground printing   The text displayed on the screen is printed, but not necessarily stored.

form completion   One task which can be more difficult to complete successfully on a word processor than on a typewriter is form filling. This is due to two main factors:

-    The printer is separate from the screen and the operator cannot easily align the print with a pre-printed form as on a typewriter.

-    Spacing on pre-printed forms does not always fall into definite categories of single, one and a half, double or treble line spacing. Although a word processor can vary line spacing at printout stage it can be difficult to align the print with the lines on existing forms.

The solution to this problem is to design a form suitable for the application required and to store it on disk, ready for in-filling with variable details when required. The in-filling can be achieved either by

-    merging two files – one containing the form and the other the variable details, eg names and addresses of customers, both of which can be stored on disk; or

-    keying-in the variable details direct onto the master form on the screen.

Software is now becoming more readily available for designing forms, protecting headings, etc so that they are not inadvertently erased.

format Layout and design of document on screen or paper.

format setting The operator enters the settings for margins, line spacing, page length, etc and must therefore be aware of the pitch size required and the size of paper for the finished document, as the printout may be different to the screen display.

formatting/initialisation All new disks must be prepared for the particular system being used. The round plastic disk (inside the square protective covering) is divided into tracks going round the disk and sectors (portions) going across it. Each track and sector is numbered and as data is stored it is indexed to provide quick access when a particular piece of work is recalled.

four-function maths Addition/subtraction/division/multiplication are now possible on an increasing number of word processing systems. Useful in the production of business documents, financial accounts, management accounts, statistical information.

friction feeders Printers which use single sheets of paper receive it either in the same way as a typewriter, by the operator inserting individual sheets when required, or from a tray/cassette holding a bulk supply of paper.

full page display A screen which is capable of displaying a full page of A4 text, ie 70 lines, at one time.

function/control keys Usually referred to as dedicated function keys and used specifically for editing and other functions, eg insert, delete, merge, format, store page, tabs. A set of four or five arrow keys may also be available specifically for movement of the cursor.

gateway An interface device which enables information to be transmitted to a terminal or workstation on a different network.

global search Searching throughout a document for a specified string of characters which may be a word, numbers or a phrase. The length of the text will depend on the system being used.

global search and replace   Searching throughout a document for a specified *string of characters* which may be a word, numbers or a phrase and replacing it with an alternative. The maximum length of text will depend on the system being used.

glossary   A collective name for standard paragraphs, used by some manufacturers.

golfball   An interchangeable round printing element, similar in appearance to a golfball, which revolves until the required letter makes contact with the paper and produces a crisp clear type – good letter quality for external use.

graphic tablet   As an alternative to a QWERTY keyboard the different functions available are displayed in rectangles on the surface of a tablet/board. In a text editing system these might enable the operator to execute a variety of commands such as changing typeface, inserting and/or deleting characters/words/lines, drawing diagrams, etc.

Instead of a keyboard the operator uses an electric stylus, which completes an electrical circuit when it is placed on the rectangle labelled with the required function on the tablet.

graphics   On a dedicated word processor this facility is used mainly for vertical and horizontal lines, but computer-based systems may allow graphs, etc to be incorporated into text.

hacking   An illegal means of accessing computer data via a telephone link using a modem or acoustic coupler.

half spacing   A printing feature allowing subscripts and superscripts to be printed half a line below or above the other text.

handshaking   A 'dialogue' between two computers or a computer and a *peripheral device,* eg a printer, which establishes that a message is passed between them to their mutual satisfaction.

hard copy   Text produced on paper is known as hard copy.

hard/forced page breaks   The soft page breaks inserted by the system may not be satisfactory to the operator who may wish to insert alternative breaks which will remain even after reformatting. It is usually only possible to shorten a page, not to lengthen it, and it must be remembered that re-pagination will alter the page breaks for subsequent pages in the document.

hard magnetic disk   Commonly referred to as a Winchester disk. Very large storage capacity. It is completely sealed within its disk drive to protect the disk surface and prevent breakage.

hard/required hyphen   A hard hyphen is used by the operator in a word which invariably has a hyphen, eg co-operative, and it is not deleted during reformatting.

hard return   A return inserted by the operator at the end of a heading, line or paragraph to ensure no other text is added at that point, ie no wraparound of following text.

hardware   The hardware components of a word processing system consist of a screen/VDU, keyboard, disk drive, memory and central processing unit.

hard-wired   An operating system contained within the word processor rather than inserted by disk. This makes impossible any update of the capabilities of the system.

header   A short piece of text printed automatically within the top margin of every page or selected pages of a multi-page document, eg title of a report. The operator determines the position of the header within the top margin and may instruct for odd and even pages to be printed in a different position if unequal margins are being used.

health   Potential problems relating to health should be considered when implementing electronic office systems. The main areas which cause concern are epilepsy, eyes, posture, radiation and stress.

help files   On some systems it is possible for the operator to request assistance when using the system by calling up a HELP menu on the screen. The operator selects the area where assistance is needed and then receives specific information to enable work to continue.

highlighting   Characters displayed in reverse video on the VDU enable the operator to see which section of text will be affected when the command is executed. Some systems highlight the cursor position to aid the operator.

home key   A cursor control key which automatically moves the cursor to the home position, ie the left screen margin on line one.

home position   The home position of the cursor is the left screen margin on line one.

hopper/sheet feeders   Single sheets of paper are held in a tray attached to the printer. On instruction from the system a single sheet of paper is fed into the printer, thus saving time when printing a multi-page text or completing a mail merge.

horizontal scroll   Word processing screens usually display 80 characters. Horizontal scroll enables the 81st character onwards to be viewed when the text moves to the left and temporarily disappears from view.

hot/soft zone   Designates the number of character spaces inside the right-hand margin of a printed line, within which wordwrap will take place automatically on identifying a space or a hyphen. Helps the operator equalise the length of lines without hyphenation.

hyphenation   Undertaken by the operator or automatically by the system – if the latter is used it will almost certainly be unacceptable. A hard hyphen is used by the operator in a word which invariably has a hyphen, eg co-operative. A soft hyphen is used by the operator or system to hyphenate a word at the end of a line. Should the text be reformatted it will disappear if no longer at a line end.

icon   Symbols on the screen which represent particular functions, eg filing cabinet, filing folders, calculator, waste bin. The required function is selected using a *mouse* and by pressing a button the selected item is activated.

ideal working position   The operator should use an adjustable chair, so that the height of the seat, with feet comfortably resting on the floor, and angle of back support can be adjusted to suit individual requirements. The keyboard should also be at a suitable height and the VDU should be adjustable and flicker free. The decor in the office should be non-reflective and lighting should be shadow-free. Each piece of equipment should be in a convenient location and there should be adequate space for papers.

impact printer   A typing element, eg daisywheel or dot matrix, strikes an ink or carbon ribbon to form an impression on the paper. A clear sharp image is produced, and carbon copies can be made.

incremental spaces   Additional spaces inserted by the system when justifying the right-hand margin.

indent   Text which is indented a specified number of spaces, eg 5, to the right of the left margin.

index/directory   Lists documents recorded on storage medium and indicates disk capacity used and that which is available.

ink jet printers   As the printer head moves across the page, electrostatic drops of ink are propelled on to the paper at high speed line by line. This is a non-impact printing technique and although relatively quiet to use, it cannot produce carbon copies.

input typing   The keying-in of text via a keyboard. Unlike a typewriter, it is unnecessary to return at the end of each line because the system will automatically carry any word which will not fit at the end of a line to the next.

insert mode   A system has to be in *insert mode* before insertions may be made into existing text.

insertion   Characters, words, lines or paragraphs of text may be inserted at any point within a document. It is advisable to reformat after inserting items to ensure that wraparound has occurred through the text.

inset paragraph   When a paragraph is to be inset from the left margin the system will treat the tab stop as a 'temporary' margin, provided the operator used the appropriate instruction, until a hard return is entered.

integral keyboard   The integral keyboard forms part of the VDU casing.

integrated software   An integrated software package enables operators to move from one application to another and transfer information from one package to another. Packages could cover applications such as word processing, financial modelling or graphics, and statistics in a spreadsheet could be converted into a graph and then inserted into a report prepared using the word processing facility.

intelligent photocopier   An advanced photocopier that can also be used as an output device for a computer system. A communications link enables multiple copies of high quality printed copy to be produced and collated automatically.

intelligent terminal   In addition to the central processing unit an intelligent terminal has some processing power of its own.

interface   Peripherals can be linked together by interfaces in the form of cables or boxes, eg several workstations may be connected to one printer.

internal/working memory   Some of the memory will be *read only* and is stored permanently on a *read only memory* chip but other information stored on a *random access memory* chip will be lost when the system is turned off.

job/log/time sheet   Operators may have to record time spent on each document to enable charge-back costing to be undertaken. This may simply be indicated as units, each unit representing, say, 10 minutes.

justification   Straight left- and right- hand margins which may be displayed on the screen or undertaken at the printing stage. The text 'spreads' between the margins by either

– varying the space between words leaving characters equally spaced, or

– varying the space between characters leaving equal space between words.

keep   It may be important to keep two pieces of text on one page, eg column headings on the same page as the columns. Insertion of the appropriate code before or after the piece of text will ensure it is retained as a single block during pagination and not divided between two pages.

key A keyboard is made up of switches labelled with a character(s) which appears on the screen when the key/switch is depressed on the keyboard.

keyboard Input device used by operators for word processing with alphanumeric and special keys to perform specific functions. Used to create and edit text and to give operating instructions to the system.

keyboard alternatives The keyboard is not the only method of instructing a computer system. The alternatives are relatively expensive, partly because the lack of demand means they are not mass produced. Examples of alternatives currently available are: graphic tablet, touch panel screen, light pen, the cat, the mouse, voice commands, freehand input.

keystroke The pressing of a single key on a keyboard to enter or edit text, to print or to input a command.

keystroke memory/user defined key Some commands require a series of keystrokes in a specific sequence to perform a task. To assist the operator there may be a memory function allowing the sequence to be stored and recalled quickly and accurately when required. Keyboards with keys such as f1 f2 f3 often provide this facility.

keyword indexing On very sophisticated word processing systems it may be possible to prepare an index or table of contents automatically by selecting and/or coding key words within a document.

kilobyte (K) (KB) (Kb) Unit of measurement of memory or disk storage capacity, eg 1K = 1000/1024 bytes or characters.

labels The contents of a disk should be summarised on a label stuck on the front of the disk. The label should be completed, whenever possible, before placing on the disk. If it is necessary to add information later a felt tip pen must be used.

laser optical disk Not commercially used, due partly to slow read/write speeds and also because it can only be used once –

erasing and overwriting is not possible. There is no danger of losing recorded data because only a beam of light is in contact with the disk, which is scanned by a minute low-power laser. There is therefore no wear and tear as there is with magnetic disks.

laser printers Printing is undertaken at very high speeds. The laser image is projected on to a piece of film which is fixed onto the paper by a method similar to that used to print photographic images. The quality of print is very high, and production is very fast because it prints a whole page in one operation – ideal for external use such as brochures and catalogues.

letter quality Describes the standard of printing and indicates that it is acceptable for use on correspondence and documentation for external distribution.

library An alternative word for a disk-based spelling dictionary.

light pen Two types, one used to input drawings and another for reading bar codes. Both are linked to a terminal by a fine cable.

line drawing (or word processing graphics) Horizontal and vertical lines used in text require a line graphics facility. Within this facility, lines are easy to draw on the screen and print on paper, providing a suitable printer is used, but are usually restricted to vertical and horizontal. This facility is useful in the production of charts, graphs, diagrams, tables, forms, schedules, etc but note

- lines may have kinks or breaks and corners may not be perfect
- printer must be capable of printing the appropriate symbols
- lines may not be displayed on the screen.

With the development of more complex word processing systems it is becoming increasingly possible to incorporate charts/graphs into documents produced on a word processor.

line ending A line end defined by the operator is indicated by a symbol representing a hard return.

line feed The movement of paper a line at a time in the printer.

line height/pitch Usually six lines per vertical inch but printers may allow this to be varied, eg eight lines per vertical inch.

line numbering This function is only found on sophisticated systems and allows the operator to number each line of text to assist the editing process. Numbering may restart on each page or continue throughout a document.

line printer Prints a line at a time at very high speed, eg ink jet printer.

line spacing Usually specified as single, one and a half or double spacing with six single lines being required for each vertical inch of paper. The screen may only display in single line spacing and variations will only appear on the printed copy.

lines per minute (lpm) Describes the speed at which a line printer operates.

liquid crystal display A display made by activating a liquid crystal substance used in flat screens on portable computers and calculators.

local area network (LAN) Information, via a cable, can be passed to a number of computers within a single site or building.

log/job/time sheet Operators may have to record time spent on each document to enable charge-back costing to be undertaken. This may simply be indicated as units, each unit representing, say, 10 minutes.

log on Entry of the date and time when initially switching on the system.

logging To assist in the control and monitoring of incoming and outgoing work, records are kept on a log (time) sheet.

logic/arithmetic unit Part of the central processing unit which performs arithmetic, eg addition and multiplication, and non-arithmetic (logic) tasks, eg sorting records.

long-term memory An external or permanent memory, eg a disk, for software programs or text.

lower case   Small letters only, ie no capitals (upper case).

machine start-up   Specific procedure required to commence operating the word processor.

magnetic media   Storage media for recording instructions or text, eg floppy disks.

mail merge   Automatic insertion of variables, eg name and address, into constant text of letter. The variable information must be stored in one document and the standard text in another. The system merges the two documents, eg name and address list with standard letter, and prints 'personal' letters automatically with minimum operator intervention. Ideally, a hopper feed attachment on the printer or continuous stationery should be available when producing a mail merge.

mailing list   Names and addresses are keyed-in giving each line a reference, so that all or selected lines may be extracted. Letters and/or envelopes would require the full name and address to be inserted/printed but it would also be possible to select customers in a specified area and ignore all others that have been stored in the document.

main memory   The operating program is stored in the main memory after the operating disk has been loaded into the system. It also stores text which is being processed.

mainframe   A large powerful computer capable of a wide range of computer applications and word processing simultaneously. Terminals are linked to the mainframe via a network and it is probably necessary to have more than one printer available.

maintenance contract   The supplier will generally encourage purchasers to enter into a maintenance contract to provide urgent repair facilities and periodical preventative maintenance.

management workstation   Managers who have a VDU on their desks will be able to access the following: personal diary, departmental calendar, reminder file, mailbox, personal files, departmental files, company files, spelling checker, abbreviation dictionary, distribution list, telephone numbers, departmental personnel records, etc; and undertake calculations, budget monitoring, creation and distribution of text, word processing for internal mail.

margins Left and right margins, which determine the length of the printed line, can be set and changed at any point within a document.

mark Marker blocks are inserted at the beginning and end of a piece of text which is to be used in a specific way, eg moving a paragraph to a new position.

maths program Some systems have a maths program which provides facilities for calculation of both horizontal and vertical columns. An additional numeric keypad may also be incorporated on the right-hand side of the keyboard.

megabytes (M) (MB) (Mb) Unit of measurement of memory or disk storage capacity, ie 1M = 1,000,000/1,024,000 bytes or characters, ie, 1000K.

memory A storage device which retains information permanently or temporarily.

memory sizes The size of the computer's memory is usually described in kilobytes, eg 64K = 64,000 bytes/characters and 128K = 128,000 bytes/characters.

menu Menus help to make the system *user friendly* by displaying sets of options on the screen to save the operator learning vast lists of commands or continually referring to a manual.

menu based systems The operator is presented with a series of options from which the next task must be selected, eg E to edit existing document, C to create new document, P to print document. The more experienced operator may have the option of using the menu provided by the software or by-passing it for quicker operation of the system.

menu-driven   Programs which present the operator with a list of choices at any particular time and which are displayed on the screen when required.

merge   Two or more text documents are combined to produce a new document, eg

- basic letter with name and address list to create a standard letter
- blank form with selected information.

merge printing   This takes place when two or more pieces of text merge at printout to create a new document, eg a standard letter.

message switching   Messages sent via communication networks are transmitted to any user, on any network, by switching between networks until the destination is reached.

messages   Draw the attention of the operator to specific situations by giving information about the system, eg disk full, printer awaiting paper, no ribbon in printer, invalid command.

microchip   Silicon chip – small piece of semi-conductor material – containing electronic components, ie memory.

microcomputer   A small computer system built round a microprocessor and having all the necessary peripherals and memory to link with other computers.

microcomputer systems with word processing software   The computer can be used for all non-word processing tasks and documents created by the word processor, eg standard letters can be merged with a name and address list, and invoices prepared on the computer can access the same list.

Advantages

- A word processing software package will often have advantages for a small business or for a department in a large company, particularly in terms of price and flexibility.

- The cost of a dedicated system could rarely be justified by the quantity of good quality typing required, but the total computing requirements for accounting, data storage, payroll, financial planning and word processing might well justify the installation of a microcomputer.

- A computer-based system is much more economical if you already have a computer or need combined computer and word processing facilities.

- Virtually all computers have word processing software available, from small home computers to large mainframe systems.

- Some computer manufacturers provide special hardware/ software combinations, with word processing as a primary consideration.

- A computer usually has more memory and disk space available, which enables more documents to be stored and processed.

Disadvantages

- Functions such as cursor movement, centring, insertion, deletion will often be possible only with multiple key strokes, rather than by using one key, unless the system has been specially 'configured' (set up by the dealer) for the chosen package. However, dealers and manufacturers are rapidly responding to the needs of the market by performing this configuration for popular packages.

- No formal training is included with a package which is bought 'off the shelf' although it will generally include a reference manual and demonstration documents/tasks.

- It is usually a slightly more complicated process to run a software package than to use a dedicated word processor, due to its need for greater flexibility, and the operator may require a little more supervision in the early stages.

- A computer is a general-purpose machine, not fixed to any one task. Compromises have therefore been made in its design in favour of computer-type work rather than word processing.

- This compromise results in a general-purpose keyboard and there could be redundant keys or keys where the label is different from the function.

- The software may not be easy to use and it may be necessary to memorise many codes and combinations of keys.

- The display could be unattractive and on some of the smaller computers the screen will not show true descenders (the part of a letter that appears below the baseline – eg q p j g).

microfiche   A sheet of microfilm with rows of images providing quick reference to a large number of documents which do not require updating, eg a catalogue of part numbers, or files no longer in frequent use.

microfilm   A favourable alternative to paper filing because of the reduced amount of space required to store the same amount of information. It is possible for computerised output to be in microfilm format instead of paper.

microprocessor   Central silicon chip containing the control unit of the computer or word processor.

minicomputer   A medium sized computer which is between a mainframe and a micro. A few terminals can be linked together sharing the central processing unit and disk drive. One or more printers may be available.

mnemonic   As an aid to remembering the meaning of a group of words the initial letters of the words form a new term, eg BASIC, ASCII.

mode   Different facilities (modes) within the software, used to insert, delete, format, etc.

modem   A **Mo**dulator-**Dem**odulator converts data from digital signals (computer output) to analog signals (telephone output) which can be sent via telephone lines. A similar device at the receiving end of the telephone line then converts the analog signals back into digital signals that can be understood by the computer.

mouse   A small hand-held device linked to the computer (used in conjunction with a keyboard) by a cable and which, when moved over a flat surface, can locate and move a pointer (cursor) on the screen. The cursor is moved rapidly around the screen allowing menu selection and manipulation of screen data. By selecting a key on the mouse a command can be executed. If text or numeric data is required a conventional keyboard must be used.

move   A piece of text which has been marked at the beginning and end is removed from one location and inserted in another.

movement of text   Vertical movement of paragraphs and, in the case of columns, horizontal movement, ie column 1 moved to position of column 3 enabling columns 2 and 3 to relocate as columns 1 and 2. The movement of text can be within a document or to another document or disk.

When text is removed from the original position and re-inserted the process is known as 'cut and paste'. Text which is copied to a new location is known as 'cut and leave'.

multi pass   Some dot matrix printers print each line twice allowing more dots to fill in the gaps and increase the print to *near letter quality*.

multi-strike ribbon   A carbon ribbon which only moves a fraction of a character at a time, thus having a much longer life span than single-strike carbon ribbons.

multi-window   The screen is able to display more than one document or task at the same time.

naming a disk   On some systems it is necessary to name a disk before opening files and/or documents whereas others are named automatically during the format procedure.

On a system requiring the disk to be named, the disk represents the filing cabinet, the file the divisions within each drawer of the filing cabinet, the documents the various documents within individual folders and pages the pages that make up the documents.

disk	filing cabinet	CONVEYANCING
file	file pockets	SALE OF 23 HIGH STREET
document	document	letters, searches, etc.
pages	pages	individual pages of text

naming and renaming files   The system may restrict the number of characters in the name of a file/document to 8 characters, and will permit the file/document to be re-named if necessary.

narrowband   A low capacity telecommunications channel.

near letter quality   Printing is not of letter quality but acceptable for most purposes.

negative values (minus)   When calculating is undertaken, negative values may be displayed on the screen in reverse video (highlighting of text) to assist the operator.

network   A system whereby a number of word processors, computers, terminals and other components such as printers and disk drives can be linked together to provide communication electronically. Sometimes networks themselves are linked together through an interface called a gateway. A local area network (LAN) enables two-way telecommunication within a company.

Networks allow different office systems to communicate via a connecting cable with frequently positioned sockets. Devices connected to the network will include workstations, printers, telephones and special communications features to permit transmission to and from other networks.

Staff undertake their work at individual independent workstations with separate facilities, eg file storage. The network link can be used to communicate with other users, to access files and peripherals that other users maintain and to access the company's main archival files and/or additional devices such as high speed printers and other networks either internally or externally.

no carbon required (NCR)   Paper which has been treated on the reverse side with a special substance produces a copy underneath when writing or printing (typing) takes place, without the need to insert carbon paper.

non-impact printers High speed printers which are very quiet in operation, but cannot produce carbon copies because no printing element strikes the paper, eg laser and ink jet printers.

numeric keypad An additional block of numeric keys – similar in appearance to a calculator – set on the extreme right of the keyboard. Very useful when keying-in figures.

operating system Software program for the word processor which controls the operations of the various input and output devices.

operator comfort The design of the VDU is very important if the operator is to work efficiently. Some VDUs may be adjusted vertically and/or horizontally to suit the operator. A control switch enables the operator to adjust the brightness of the display but it may be necessary to attach an anti-glare filter to the screen if reflection is a problem. The height of the chair seat and position of back support should also be adjustable. A remote keyboard is preferred to allow choice of position.

operator training Suppliers generally provide only 1 – 2½ days' training programme for each operator, the cost being built into the purchase price of the equipment. This is usually inadequate and therefore 'in-house' training is necessary. The average time for operators to become proficient is three months and it is essential for managers to appreciate this to avoid the 'expectation gap'. Training should include:

- creating, revising, printing, storing, retrieving and up-dating text
- devising and maintaining an efficient filing and indexing system
- devising and maintaining efficient housekeeping procedures
- using system with care to protect health and ensure safety
- ensuring that the system is maintained in working order.

optical character recognition (OCR) This technique enables a page of text to be *read* directly into a computer or word processor and then edited as required – eliminating the need to key-in text already in printed form. The typed material must be prepared in a font which the optical character reader can recognise, ideally using a carbon film ribbon to produce a good black print.

optical character recognition reader   Text is fed into an OCR reader unit where a reading head scans the characters and converts them into digital form. It can scan an A4 page in a few seconds and transfer it either directly to the screen of the word processor or to a disk for storage until required.

Using it as an input device for word processing frees the word processor from redundant keyboarding, saves time and reduces or eliminates bottlenecks. Possible transcription errors during input are avoided and the error rate even for basic OCRs is estimated to be one per 25,000 characters.

originating ideas   Thoughts which are translated into words through either dictation, writing or a keyboard.

orphan line   The last line of a paragraph which is carried on its own to the next page.

output   Information which a system *writes to* a VDU, printer or storage device.

overstrike   The typing of two characters in one unit of space to create a character/symbol which does not have a single key on the keyboard, eg S and an oblique to form a dollar sign if $ is not available.

overtype mode   Keying-in text over existing text, with the insert mode off, deletes original text and is an easy means of correcting errors.

overwriting of disks   Disks can be protected by using the notch on the right-hand edge of the flexible disk. 8″ disks require this notch to be left uncovered but 5¼″ disks require the notch to be covered with the special write-protect labels supplied in each box of disks purchased.

overwriting of text   Revised text erases earlier version when it is stored.

package   Software purchased to use on a specific computer system.

packet switching   A technical process whereby computers control packets of data being transmitted along a network.

page   Text contained on one sheet of paper or one screenful of text.

page based system   Each page keyed-in is individually stored and may be printed at any time. Page endings are determined by the operator and although it is easy to find a particular page of text it is more difficult to move text within a document.

page break   The system or the operator inserts a code to indicate the end of a page. This instructs the printer to eject the current page if single sheets are being used, or to continue after the perforations with continuous stationery.

page display   A screen displaying between 50 and 70 lines of text and usually 80 characters per line at any one time – equivalent to a page of A4.

page numbering   The operator may enter page numbers manually but it is better for the system to enter these while printing the document as it automatically allows for any repagination undertaken. The position of the page number is defined by the operator and can be at the top or bottom of the page, left or right margin, or centre point between the margins.

page offset   A print instruction for printing to commence a specified number of spaces to the right of the set left margin, without the need to reformat. Line length is not affected as the text is simply moved across the page – particularly appropriate for pages printed on both sides where a constant wide left margin is required for binding purposes.

page printer   A whole page is assembled in the internal memory of the system and printed at high speed in one operation, eg a laser printer.

pagination   The system divides a lengthy document into pages of a specified length, eg 57 lines. If a new page is required at any point within the document a page eject instruction must be inserted before the text for the new page. It is also possible to insert codes to prevent paragraph/column headings and paragraph/column details being split on separate pages.

parallel printer interface   A wide ribbon-type cable is used to connect a printer to a computer. The most commonly known parallel interface is a Centronics. Before purchasing a printer it is essential to check the type of interface on the computer and whether an alternative can be used.

part-page display   A screen displaying between 16 and 24 lines of text and usually 80 characters per line at any one time.

password   It is easy to alter inadvertently the contents of a disk, and the possibility of unauthorised alteration should not be overlooked. For this reason, some systems incorporate a password facility which can be implemented to protect the whole disk. Thereafter unless the correct password is entered when requested by the system, the relevant file will not be retrieved into working memory.

percentage calculations   Percentages may be calculated when a suitable maths program is used.

peripheral   Any part of a computer system which is linked to the central processing unit for input, output, storage, display or transmission of text, eg keyboard, disk drive, printer.

permanent memory   An external or long-term memory, eg a disk, for software programs or text.

petal printer   Alternative name for a daisywheel printer.

phototypesetter   A device which produces the original for litho printing. Output is in the form of a photographic film suitable for printing in a number of typefaces and sizes. At the input stage of text and/or graphics, phototypesetters resemble advanced word processors with keyboard, memory and screen. Originals of printed information can be laid out and modified at speed. If a phototypesetter is linked directly to a word processor the whole procedure is streamlined. The traditional methods of printing are changing with the new technology – just as word processing is changing typing.

phrase storage   Short pieces of frequently used text may be stored, checked and recalled simply by, eg pressing two keys PASTE 1. A complimentary close is an example of a useful phrase which is keyed-in, checked only once and used many times, eg

Yours faithfully
John Smith & Co

J K Brown
Sales Manager

pica   A printing pitch which produces 10 characters per horizontal inch.

picture (image) input   Diagrams, illustrations, forms, etc are scanned by a special camera and transferred to a VDU where they can then be edited or incorporated with text or data to produce a new document.

pitch   Number of characters printed per horizontal inch, eg

10 characters to 1″/25 mm   pica
12 characters to 1″/25 mm   élite
15 characters to 1″/25 mm   micro

pixels   An abbreviation for *picture elements*. Characters on the screen are made up of tiny dots (pixels). The quality of the screen display is determined by the number of pixels on the screen and a high resolution screen provides the best viewing results for the operator.

place markers   Place markers set within a document while keying-in enable the operator to return quickly to that position later. In a lengthy report place markers might occur at the start of each section.

platen   The rubber covered cylinder around which the paper is placed in the printer.

plotter   A special attachment which enables the operator to draw on the screen or to print out diagrams.

pollution Computers can easily be damaged by pollution of various kinds and in the area around the equipment smoking, eating and drinking should be strictly forbidden. Dust can also cause an enormous amount of damage and vacuum cleaners, rather than carpet sweepers, should be used regularly.

port Position where an electrical connection can be made with the central processor in the computer.

posture Desks should be of an appropriate height and the screen and keyboard should be separate so that the operator can arrange the most suitable position, height and angle. Seat height and back position of chair should be adjustable.

pressure feed Small rubber rollers feed the paper around the platen into the printer, as on a typewriter.

Prestel The first commercial viewdata service in the world. Viewdata involves storing textual and graphical information in colour on a computer. It is easy to use – simply press buttons on a key-pad as directed through the menus to obtain the required information. Prestel is charged on a 'pay as you use' basis, but not all 'pages' of information cost the same.

print control characters Printing instructions may be displayed on the screen or hidden from the operator.

print pause While printing is taking place it is possible to pause to change a daisywheel, replace the printer ribbon, remove crumpled paper, etc and then continue printing from the point where the pause commenced.

print queue Documents to be printed are listed in order of priority and printed automatically when the printer is available, allowing the operator to continue with other tasks. This is particularly necessary when several operators share a printer and/or the printer is not located near the operator.

printer A peripheral necessary to produce printed (hard) copy of text.

printer attachments Paper is fed into the printer automatically by either a sheet feeder with single cut sheets of paper or a tractor feeder with continuous stationery.

An acoustic cover positioned over the printer reduces the noise of printing and is particularly useful on impact printers.

printing a page Most systems allow the operator to select part of a document for printing, eg page 3 when there are 15 pages in the document, without the need to print all preceding pages. If this facility is unavailable the portion should be marked and transferred to a new document which can then be printed.

printing density The number of characters printed per horizontal inch, also known as pitch.

printing on headed paper The default one inch top margin may not be sufficient for company letterheads and it will be necessary to undertake one of the following:

– change the default top margin to allow for the extra space
– insert additional blank lines before the start of each letter
– physically turn the paper up additional line spaces before printing commences.

program Software (operating instructions) which enables the system to perform specific tasks, depending on the program being used.

program disk Contains the system/operating instructions (program).

programmed key sequence If a command requires several key strokes it may be possible to define a specific key to undertake this function, eliminating the need for multiple key strokes and the possibility of error.

programmer A person who decides how a system may best perform a task and then writes a suitable program.

prompts Draw the attention of the operator to specific situations which usually require action, eg press Y to continue, press EXIT when editing complete, press P to print document.

proof reader A person who checks that the hard copy of the text is correct.

proof reading Checking that a document does not contain spelling, grammatical, punctuation or typographical errors. It is essential that all correspondence, reports and memoranda are free of errors to maintain a good impression of the company. The speed with which this can be achieved will increase with practice.

Proof reading involves four basic steps:
- Look at the document as a whole – is the layout on the page correct? Has it been formatted correctly?
- Scan the document for glaring errors. Are there any obvious typographical errors, spacing errors or have any words been incorrectly divided at the end of a line?
- Read through the entire document for meaning. Do the contents make sense? Check for grammatical errors.
- Check particularly any names, addresses or figures.

Techniques:
- Give your full attention to the document being read and, if necessary, proof read a second time.
- Place the original document and the copy side by side and use a finger from each hand to run down both documents simultaneously.
- Enlist the aid of a colleague to check charts, tables, legal documents or any other technical items.

proportional spacing A defined unit of space is allocated for each character depending on the character, eg **i** uses less space than **w**. This is popular with word processing as it gives a 'printed' appearance to a document.

protect a document Shared resources usually make some form of text protection necessary and the software program must have this facility. The level of protection does not have to be the same for all files and one user may have different levels of access for different files. Access may be available in the following ways:

- *write protected documents* allow access by any user or operator, but prevent editing and deletion;
- *copy protected documents* allow access by any user or operator, but prevent editing, deletion and copying;
- *read protected documents* can only be accessed by authorised users using the correct password;
- *unlisted documents* do not show on the disk contents and in addition authorised users require the correct password.

protected/required space   When keying-in names, figures, dates, etc it is inadvisable to divide at line ends in an inappropriate place. Division using the wraparound facility may not automatically divide at a suitable point. To overcome this, a protected space is used instead of a normal space. This has the effect of making the characters into 'one' word which wraparound will not separate and which justifying also treats as a single word. This is usually a very simple procedure such as hold CODE key while pressing space bar.

Without protected spaces:

> *It was announced recently in the Press that on 28 December 1986 Messrs A B Gray of Bristol and H J Jones of Taunton were awarded £14 856 and £7 542 respectively. A denial was printed on 3 January 1987. It was not Mr A B Gray but Mr B B Guy of Bristol, and the sum awarded was not £14 856 but £140 865.*

With protected spaces:

> *It was announced recently in the Press that on 28 December 1986 Messrs A B Gray of Bristol and H J Jones of Taunton were awarded £14 856 and £7 542 respectively. A denial was printed on 3 January 1987. It was not Mr A B Gray but Mr B B Guy of Bristol, and the sum awarded was not £14 856 but £140 865.*

protocol   A set of rules governing the transmission and reception of text from one system to another.

public switched telephone network (PSTN)   Standard telephone
service available to private and business users.

purchasing a word processing system   There are three main points
to be considered:

- Feasibility study to decide whether the anticipated workload
  justifies the expense.
- Market research to find the sources available to advise on the
  most appropriate system, and possible suppliers.
- Staff involvement in discussions and decision making associated
  with proposed purchase.

Although suppliers will be very willing to demonstrate equipment it
is very beneficial, before ordering, to visit firms currently using the
same system for the same type of work, to establish advantages and
disadvantages.

qualifications   Word processing qualifications fall into two main
categories:

- certificates of competency on particular equipment gained from
  courses organised by suppliers;
- nationally recognised examining board qualifications, eg Pitman
  and Royal Society of Arts, which may be based on practical skills
  only or combined with theoretical knowledge of word
  processing.

queue   Documents to be printed are listed in order of priority and
printed automatically when the printer is available, allowing the
operator to continue with other tasks. This is particularly necessary
when several operators share a printer and/or the printer is not
located near the operator.

QWERTY keyboard   Standard typewriter keyboard used for keying-
in text, editing, etc.

radiation   VDUs emit low levels of radiation – like a colour
television set – and equipment is available to monitor these levels.
There is no firm evidence to suggest that radiation from a VDU is a
health hazard.

ragged right margin   Text which is unjustified provides an uneven (ragged) right margin.

random access memory (RAM)   Working memory of word processor into which application programs can be *written to* or *read from* and which are loaded from outside, eg a disk.

read   Retrieving a document from file memory into working memory.

read only memory (ROM)   Permanent memory (firmware) which has been hardwired into the hardware and which cannot be changed by the operator.

read-write head   The component within the disk drive which reads data from and writes data to the disk.

re-arranging disk index/directory   This is necessary when a document is created, deleted or re-named. Some systems do this automatically but others require the operator to update.

reclaim disk space   Deletion of documents sometimes leaves unused gaps on a disk until a special program is used to re-arrange the documents and thus reclaim the vacant disk space.

record fields – fixed and variable   Each records file contains a number of sorting categories known as fields. These fields separate the information contained in each records file, eg name, address, age, so that the record fields may be selected and/or sorted according to those specific criteria. Once a records file is defined the variable details may be keyed-in and stored on disk. Note that:

- A fixed-length field requires all fields to contain the same number of character spaces.
- A variable-length field does not require all fields to contain the same number of character spaces, thus permitting the length of the field to vary according to the information contained in it.

recording equipment faults   A system should be set up for an operator to record faults when they occur. Basic checks should be undertaken to ensure there is not a poor connection, operator fault, disk fault, end of printer ribbon, etc before telephoning the service engineer.

records file   Useful in the maintenance of personnel records, mailing lists, customer information, etc. Once records have been created they are stored on the system's storage media and then displayed on the screen, printed out, or merged with other documents.

records processing   Permits the manipulation of separate items of information (fields) stored by the system in a single document (records file). Records processing may be in the form of the sorting of a records file, the selection of fields from a records file, or the simultaneous sorting and selection of fields from a records file.

reformatting or re-arrangement of text   An instruction to the system to re-arrange text after editing or revision of margins, page length, printing pitch, etc to ensure that all lines and pages fit within the settings specified. It is good practice to reformat text immediately prior to storing on disk.

rehyphenate   Reformatting text in any way will result in a change in line endings. Rehyphenation will therefore be necessary as discretionary hyphens will have disappeared and new ones may be required.

remote keyboard   A keyboard connected to the VDU by a cable, enabling the operator to select the most suitable position for both screen and keyboard.

rename   Document names may be changed at any time either before or after text has been stored.

repagination   Text is re-arranged into 'new pages' after editing.

repeat character key   The majority of word processing keyboards are designed so that any key which is depressed firmly will repeat until pressure is released. This is very useful when underscoring, drawing lines, or using the full stop for continuous dotted lines on a form.

report format   A new document is created to list all selected details from a records file. A standard letter may have been despatched to many customers and a summary is required for office and sales staff. The new document would refer to the letter and summarise addressee details in columns

LETTER TO ALL SALES MANAGERS IN AVON ON ... (DATE)

Company Name   *Address*   *Individual*   *Telephone No*

The telephone number would not have appeared on the letter, but will be required when follow-up is undertaken.

required/hard hyphen   A hard hyphen used by the operator in a word which invariably has a hyphen, eg co-operative. It is not deleted during reformatting.

required page break   A specific page end code inserted by the operator. It is not deleted if repagination is undertaken.

required/protected space   When keying-in names, figures, dates, etc it is inadvisable to divide at line ends in an inappropriate place. Division using the wraparound facility may not automatically divide at a suitable point. To overcome this, a protected space is used instead of a normal space. This has the effect of making the characters into 'one' word which wraparound will not separate and which justifying also treats as a single word. This is usually a very simple procedure such as hold CODE key while pressing space bar. See entry under **protected space** for examples.

response time   The time a system takes to react to a command.

retention period   A specified period of time that a document should be retained on disk before it can be deleted.

return   The 'carriage' return key may be used as a command to execute an instruction.

reverse video   Highlights text being edited on a screen by reversing normal colour scheme, eg black text on white background becomes white on black.

reversible disks Text is stored on both sides of the disk but the disk has to be removed and turned over to use the reverse side because it is used in a single-head disk drive.

revision tracking An author may wish to see exactly where each editing function occurred within a document and on some systems this can be recorded and viewed on screen or paper. The document can also be printed out in its final version without any of the changes being visible.

ribbons Impact printers require either fabric ribbons, which are used until the ink becomes too faint, or carbon ribbons which are used only once, give a clear, crisp consistent print and arc ideal when text is to be reproduced on a photocopier or offset-litho machine.

right justify tab Text is entered to the left of the tab stop resulting in the line endings being justified on the tab setting.

routine cleaning Each operator should be responsible for keeping all surfaces of the equipment clean and dust free.

ruler cursor In addition to the cursor in the text an additional cursor may be displayed on the ruler line indicating the horizontal column position of the cursor in the text.

ruler/scale line Usually positioned underneath the status line showing the current left and right margins and tab setting symbols, according to the type of tab used.

L --------------- ! --------------- ! --------------- ! --------------- £ --------------- £ --------------- R

rulers With the aid of a special word processing ruler, document formats may be worked out in relation to the printing pitch, page size, etc.

running corrections Corrections made by the operator to errors which occur during creation or editing of text.

save Text stored in the computer's memory is transferred to disk.

saving rulers and formats An operator may have a facility to set rulers (margins and tabs), page lengths, line spacing, etc, for recall whenever required. If the operator has several groups of files, eg LETTERS, MEMOS, REPORTS, MINUTES, and within each there is a *standard template*, each document within a group is automatically set up with the rulers and formats required.

scale/ruler line Usually positioned underneath the status line. Shows the current left and right margins and tab setting symbols, according to the type of tab used.

L---------------!---------------!---------------!---------------£---------------£---------------R

screen Displays the text being created or revised and information to assist the operator. It is also known as the visual display unit (VDU). Characters are displayed by means of a cathode ray tube. Common screen colours are green, white or amber on a dark background and the degree of brightness can be adjusted by the operator.

screen-based No hard copy of the text is either available or required.

screen display Text may or may not be in the same format on the screen as the printed version – depends on the system being used.

screen sizes

40-column	screen is 40 characters wide
80-column	screen is 80 characters wide
quarter-page	16-24 lines of text displayed on 40 column screen
half-page	16-24 lines of text displayed on 80 column screen
full-page	50-70 lines of text displayed on 80 column screen

scroll Moving text vertically or horizontally on the VDU to enable the whole document to be read in sections according to the size of the screen capacity.

search and replace The operator is able to change a string of characters throughout part or whole of a document with an alternative string, eg 'electric' replaced with 'electronic'. The system highlights and stops at the first occurrence of the word and the operator changes and/or instructs the system to proceed to the next occurrence. If the original string of characters is automatically replaced by the revised string then this procedure is known as *global search and replace.*

security copy   An alternative term for the back-up copy of a disk.

security systems   Overall security procedures in the organisation should be re-examined. Privacy of information in the system needs to be protected through software control as well as the physical protection of terminals and storage media.

It is easy to alter inadvertently the contents of a disk and the possibility of unauthorised alteration should not be overlooked. For this reason, some systems incorporate a password facility which can be implemented to protect the whole disk. Thereafter, unless the correct password is entered when requested by the system, the relevant file will not be retrieved into working memory.

A secure area will be needed to store back-up copies of disks which can be used to recreate an information base if anything goes wrong with the current disk.

selecting records   When records are selected, a number of records are usually extracted from the entire file according to criteria specified by the operator, eg

- select 'clients' who live in a specific town   *or*
- select 'products' with a specific code   *or*
- select clients in a specific town who owe over £500   *or*
- select all products with a specific code sold after a stated date.

selective printing   Many systems enable the operator to print selected pages within a document, eg in a 15 page document only to print pages 9 and 10.

sequential/serial access   Information is read from the storage medium, eg tape, in sequence until the required portion is reached. This is a very slow method of finding the text required.

serial printer interface   The printer is connected to the computer via a cable and a serial communication port which transmits instructions as single *bits* of information which the computer can understand. The most commonly known serial interface is an RS232C. Before purchasing a printer it is essential to check the type of interface on the computer and whether an alternative can be used.

service codes The operator is provided with codes to indicate bold print, end of paragraph, end of unit, change of pitch, etc and may choose to have these permanently displayed within the text or only during final proof reading.

shared-facilities system Several workstations and/or terminals, which may have their own central processing unit, share the other components/facilities of the system, ie printer and disk storage.

shared logic Configuration whereby multiple workstations in a system are connected to a single processing unit which provides the processing power, storage and printing capability for a large number of operators at the same time. The central processing unit and the memory are shared.

shared resources Two or more workstations, each having their own central processing unit, share a printer and disk storage.

short-term/temporary memory An internal memory which is lost when the system is turned off.

single density disks This refers to the density at which characters are stored within each sector and track on the disk.

single element print fonts (heads) Single element printing heads, eg golfball/daisywheel/thimble, contain all the characters which may be keyed-in from the keyboard and may be made of plastic or metal. They should be stored in a protective case when not in use and if a particular style of print is required a duplicate font should always be in stock as a broken character renders the font useless.

single-head disk drive This type of disk drive is necessary when single sided or reversible disks are used to enable access to the disk.

single line display Electronic typewriters may have a single line display which indicates each time a character is entered by displaying it on the right-hand side of the line, moving previous characters to the left.

single sheet feed   A tray attached to the printer contains single sheets of paper which are fed into the printer as required.

single sided disks   Text is stored on one side of the disk only and a single-head disk drive is used.

single strike ribbon   A high quality ribbon which produces an excellent print-out but is rather expensive as it is only used once.

skeleton letter   A standard letter which only requires the name and address of the recipient to be inserted.

soft copy   Text displayed on the screen, and which may be stored in the memory, but for which there is no hard copy.

soft/discretionary hyphen   A hyphen may be inserted to divide a word at a line-end to improve the appearance of the text. If the line length is altered the hyphen will disappear if no longer appropriate.

soft/hot zone   Designates the number of character spaces inside the right-hand margin of a printed line, within which wordwrap will take place automatically on identifying a space or hyphen. Helps the operator equalise the length of lines without hyphenation.

soft page breaks   A page end inserted by the system, as specified in the format instructions, but which will be removed if not required when text is repaginated.

soft return   A return inserted by the system to enable wraparound to take place, but which will be removed if not required during editing or reformatting.

software   Program or string of instructions to the workstation enabling it to perform as a word processor.

software copyright   Unlimited copying of software is illegal, although a reasonable number of copies for back-up purposes by the purchaser is permissible.

sorting records   Records can be sorted into alphabetical or numerical, ascending (A-Z 1-10) or descending (Z-A 10-1) order.

special characters   Characters on the keyboard which are not alphabetical or numerical, eg £ & ( ) , .

speech recognition   Computer input is by means of the operator's spoken words.

speech synthesis   Computer output is by simulated speech.

spelling check   Text may be checked by running a spelling program. Any unrecognised words are highlighted for the operator's attention. Spelling correction should be fast, but on a floppy disk system searching through a long document can be very time-consuming. It is a useful facility for technical data but careful proof reading may be better.

spelling dictionary   The dictionary itself must be accurate. The size of the dictionary can affect the usefulness of this facility and on a floppy disk system the storage space available for a comprehensive dictionary is limited. Specialist or technical vocabulary can be incorporated into the dictionary by the operator.

spinwriter/thimble   An interchangeable cone-shaped printing element which rotates and prints at a similar speed to a daisywheel.

split screen   The operator can display two or more different parts of a document on the screen at the same time, and work within each section independently.

sprocket/tractor feeder   An attachment on a printer which is necessary when continuous stationery is used – usually on a dot matrix printer. Two circular belts with protruding studs, one each side of the printer, catch and feed the paper.

stand-alone   Single independent workstation comprising keyboard, screen, storage unit, memory and central processing unit. A **single-station** system has its own printer, usually a separate unit connected by a cable, but on a **multi-station** system the printer is shared with other workstations. This means that two or more workstations can undertake different tasks, using the printer only when needed. Only one person can use each workstation, but if it has foreground/ background capabilities it can undertake more than one task at once. Stand-alone does not necessarily mean alienated – via a suitable communications link, each workstation can be connected to other systems and none of its stand-alone capabilities are impaired.

standard letters   The basic letter is keyed-in and stored, then merged with names and addresses automatically or semi-automatically when required.

–   Automatic insertion of variables into constant text of letter requires the names and addresses to be stored in one document and the standard letter in another. By merging the two documents the system produces standard letters with minimum operator intervention. Automatic printing will then take place (mail merge). The name and address document can of course be used for envelopes or labels.

–   Semi-automatic (manual) insertion of variables into constant text of letter requires the standard letter to be recalled to the screen with codes inserted at predetermined points to allow the operator to key-in manually the variable information.

standard paragraph   Text which is stored ready to be used in a variety of documents and is combined with other standard text or variable text as required.

standard template   The operator sets rulers (margins and tabs), line and character pitch, line spacing, page lengths, page numbering, etc and stores on disk for recall when opening a new document. The system may permit individual templates to be stored on each disk for different types of work, eg letters, reports, quotations. The template could also include standard text.

standard typewriter keys   Commonly known as the QWERTY keyboard. Necessary when keying-in or editing text but may also be used as non-dedicated function keys when combined with a function key.

standard words and phrases   Date/reference/salutation/ complimentary close etc and frequently used paragraphs may be stored on disk and recalled whenever required.

starting-up the system   After switching on the system, the system disk is inserted into the appropriate disk drive. The software program is transferred from the disk to the internal memory, taking only a few seconds to complete.

static Static electricity can build up in the atmosphere, particularly where man-made fibres are used extensively, and can lead to the operator receiving small shocks from the equipment or to a malfunction of the system.

stationery Single sheets of paper or continuous stationery are required to produce hard copies of text stored on disk.

status/control line Shows the state of the work in progress, eg

- disk drive containing the working disk
- name of file and/or document
- current tasks being undertaken by the system
- current page number in document and number of pages already stored
- position of the cursor on the screen, specified as a horizontal line number and position within screen margins
- line spacing, printing pitch and page length, used when printing text. For example:

  A:PROBATE:JENKINS   Editing Text   Page 5 line 10 of 55 Col 13 Layout   Pitch 12   Line Spacing 2   Line Pitch 6

stop code A character or symbol inserted in the text to indicate the position for inserting variable information.

storage Information is retained in the memory in a form which is understood by the computer.

storage of documents/files Each document stored must be given a reference/name for future use so that it can be recalled for amendment or printing.

stress Eye strain and body fatigue cannot be separated from mental fatigue or stress. Operators should have adequate regular breaks from the VDU, eg work no longer than two hours continuously, and relief periods between work spells should be of at least 20 minutes. Noise level should be reduced as much as possible, eg acoustic hood on printer, adjustment of volume of phone bells. Pleasant decor and the convenient positioning of equipment, supplies and materials will help to provide an attractive, restful and comfortable working environment.

string   A series of alphabetic/numeric/additional characters.

subscript   Characters appear below the baseline in a line of printed text, eg H_2O.

superscript   Characters appear above the baseline in a line of printed text, eg m^2.

supervisor   If there are more than three operators, consideration should be given to appointing a supervisor to oversee the operation. A good word processing supervisor is a special person requiring the following:

- diplomacy and tact
- ability to get on with people
- management skills
- ability to reconcile the conflicting needs of employers and employees
- composure under pressure
- a good working knowledge of the capabilities and limitations of the system used
- natural leadership qualities
- ability to keep everybody happy and still produce the work.

system   In a computing context this is a combination of hardware and software designed to produce the desired result, eg word processing.

system disk   A software disk containing a word processing program. Must be inserted and read into the memory before the operator can commence work.

systems analyst   Person trained to analyse business procedures who recommends and liaises with the programmer when clerical systems are computerised.

tab   A tab key moves the cursor instantly to a predetermined tab setting, eliminating the need to tap the space bar continuously or to use the cursor.

tab settings   Tabs may be set for a variety of different purposes:

- ordinary tab for general column work or indented paragraphs
- inset tab for insetting a piece of text from the left margin
- decimal tab for aligning columns of money
- centre tab for centring a heading or column
- right justify tab for aligning column with straight right side.

teleconferencing   A cost-effective means of conducting meetings when travel and time costs are high. The most basic method is by telephone but video, facsimile transmission and database access can also be used. Meetings may be recorded for re-viewing at a later date if required.

telesoftware   Computer programs sent via the telephone line or as part of the television teletext signal. A suitable decoder enables the computer program to be entered directly into the memory of a computer and then 'run'.

teletex   An electronic mail service whereby word processors, electronic typewriters or other terminals can be connected to the teletex service to operate over the telephone or telex network. Transmission is much faster than ordinary telex.

Documents can be keyed-in, corrected and amended before being transmitted in normal typewritten style, including upper and lower case characters. Work being undertaken on the screen is not interrupted when incoming messages are received, or when outgoing messages are dialled and transmitted.

teletext   An information service sent as part of the broadcast television signal, CEEFAX on BBC and ORACLE on IBA. With a suitable decoder, ie a television with built-in teletext capability or a separate decoder, the information can be displayed on the television screen as a series of pages.

telex   Telex is an acronym for ***tele***printer ***ex***change. It transmits typed messages from one location to another providing two-way

telecommunication. Apart from a QWERTY keyboard there is a
printer and a dialling unit and on modern equipment a screen and
memory facility which may be connected to the company computer
or word processor. Connection is usually available 24 hours a day
with direct subscriber dialling.

temperature   Computer systems require a comfortable working
temperature, without extremes of heat or cold, if performance is not
to be affected by the atmospheric conditions.

temporary/short-term memory   An internal memory which is lost
when the system is turned off.

tenosynovitis   Inflammation of the tendon sheaths in the fingers,
wrists and elbows is known by various names including 'typist's
cramp' and 'tennis elbow'. Nerves are also affected and can carry the
pain all through the arm. Tenosynovitis is a crippling disease
restricting movement of the hand and/or arm and may prevent
gripping or twisting, eg turning taps and opening bottles.

Symptoms range from a tingling in the fingers to pain and swelling
in the knuckles, wrists and elbows, and come on quickly after
starting to type and usually only disappear after a night's rest.

The cause appears to be the continual speed with which an
electronic keyboard is used, often in excess of 100 wpm and 10,000
key depressions an hour, and the design of the QWERTY keyboard.
Operator comfort, regular breaks and a variation of work will help to
reduce the possibility of this problem developing.

terminal   A micro or mainframe may have a number of terminals,
consisting of a VDU and keyboard, situated throughout a company,
giving access to the memory of the computer and providing input
and output of information.

A terminal which is controlled solely by a system's central
processing unit is known as a *dumb terminal*. If the terminal has
some processing power of its own it is known as an *intelligent
terminal*.

text   A general term for words, numbers and symbols which have
been used to create documents of all kinds on a word processor.

text assembly   The use of standard words, phrases or paragraphs to compile a single document. An operator assembles a 'new' document by retrieving from storage words, phrases or paragraphs in any order specified. This is often referred to as *boilerplating*.

Each selection will be identified by a symbol, number or name and may have to be stored in a separate document. Each selection is retrieved from memory in the specified order and automatically assembled by the system into a new document. Names, addresses, etc can be keyed-in to complete the document prior to printing. Checking time and the possibility of vital information being omitted or incorrectly typed is reduced. Assembly may take place on the screen or during printing.

text author   A text author provides work for the word processor operator/secretary to undertake. The following information must be supplied to the operator, preferably on a standard pre-printed *work request form* (see page 81), to ensure work is completed satisfactorily:

- draft, top copy, internal or external use
- number of originals and photocopies required
- line spacing and typestyle if choice is available
- turnaround time
- indication of length of time to be retained on disk
- any special requirements
- degree of confidentiality

text author training   Training will involve how to handle text for processing in accordance with standard procedures, eg

- knowing the capabilities and limitations of the system
- producing work for text creation (dictation and/or handwritten)
- revising hard copy which has already been created and stored
- giving adequate instructions for the storage and retrieval of text.

A maximum number of permitted drafts should be set to avoid endless careless drafting. Authors need to understand that text still has to be entered via the keyboard and this initial entry is only marginally faster than on a typewriter.

A useful part of the training process can be to arrange demonstrations to show the system's capabilities to text authors and management. Using the operators for these demonstrations will increase their confidence and benefit potential users of the system.

text copied/reproduced   Text which is copied to a new location but also remains in the original position may be referred to as *cut and leave* or *copy block.*

text creation   Before text can be keyed-in on a word processor a document must be created on the storage medium (usually a disk) to receive the text and to enable it to be recalled on later occasions.

text printing   One or more copies of individual pages or complete documents may be printed. Using a print queue enables the operator to specify documents to be printed and their order. The system prints the first document, then the next, until all printing tasks are complete without disturbing the foreground work. If several operators have to share a printer then a 'queue' for the printer will form and each operator's work will be printed according to their position in the queue.

The screen may display text only in single line spacing but this may be altered when text is printed. Some systems display text according to the line spacing specified by the operator. To vary line spacing within a document it is necessary to insert appropriate codes at the beginning and end of the specified piece of text.

text processor   An electronic typewriter which has been upgraded with a screen and disk drive to enable word processing tasks to be undertaken.

text/word processing   Typing, editing, storing, printing and communicating text with the aid of a computer.

Particularly useful as a means of text production when handling the following types of documents:

- Repetitive text   standard and circular letters
- Multi-draft   client reports and magazine articles
- Constructed   standard letters and legal documents
- Periodic   price lists, telephone directories, sales or financial reports
- High quality   makes full use of special typing and printing facilities.

thermal printer   A silent non-impact printer producing good quality print on expensive heat-sensitive paper.

thimble/spinwriter   An interchangeable cone-shaped printing element which prints at a similar speed to a daisywheel.

thin window display   A single-line display of between 15-40 characters used to display text on electronic typewriters.

time/job/log sheet   Operators may have to record time spent on each document to enable charge-back costing to be undertaken. This may simply be indicated as units, each unit representing, say, 10 minutes.

time-sharing   Powerful computer facilities shared between a number of users (individuals or companies) at the same time on different terminals.

toggle switch   An instruction which is the same to initiate as to terminate, eg after pressing the shift lock characters appear in upper case but on pressing it again the characters will be in lower case.

top margin   The space at the top of the page before printing commences.

touch panel screen   A number of options displayed in specific positions on the screen only require touch to indicate to the system which the user requires. There are two main types of screen:

- A special display screen consisting of two layers each containing an invisible mesh of very fine wires. The outer layer is flexible. When it is touched by the finger, the light pressure brings it into contact with the other layer and an electrical circuit is formed.

- An alternative screen contains an invisible mesh of criss-crossed light beams. As the operator's finger touches the screen it breaks the grid and the system knows exactly where the finger is.

tracks   Magnetic disks are divided into tracks for storing data, in a similar way to gramophone records.

tractor/sprocket feeder   An attachment on a printer which is necessary when continuous stationery is used – usually on a dot matrix printer. Two circular belts with protruding studs, one each side of the printer, catch and feed the paper.

training   Operators must receive adequate training if equipment is to be used efficiently and as quickly as possible. Training may be undertaken by the supplier, local college, or private training organisation. After some staff have been trained a company may prefer future training to be 'in-house'.

training manual   Equipment manuals are rarely adequate and sometimes totally unsuitable for operator use and a word processing supervisor may have to rewrite in easy steps with clear instructions. Operators can progress through the manual, learning more advanced functions as and when their expertise develops and/or their work requires more knowledge and understanding.

transcription   The keying-in of manuscript, audio and/or shorthand dictation on to a word processor which is then returned to the author in printed format.

transmission   Transmitting text to another word processor or computer by means of a communication channel.

turnaround time   Time taken to key-in, proof read, correct, print and return a document to the originator.

typeface/typestyle   Particular style of character(s) – most typefaces have a name, eg Courier and Cubic. Variation can be achieved by changing the single element printing head or by inserting appropriate codes for a dot matrix printer. Some systems enable the operator to change the size and/or style of print during printing. It is advisable to check styles available when selecting which printer to buy. A facility to 'hold' and then 'resume' printing must be available if a print head has to be changed during the printing of a document.

typing manual   This will set out details of company house style (if standard style used) relating to finished tasks, eg paper used, margins, block or indented paragraphs, open or standard punctuation. Operators and text authors should both be aware of this information.

typographical   Refers to characters originated on a keyboard.

unattended printing   Printing which is undertaken using continuous stationery or a hopper feed and thus does not require the operator to be present.

underscoring   May be keyed-in as on a typewriter, simultaneously as text is entered, or by instruction to underscore specific portions of text. Some systems will display underscoring on screen, others only indicate it is required by a code and the effect is not seen until printing has taken place.

undo   An operator may inadvertently make errors when text editing and wish to recall the document in its previous form. Many systems allow the operator to 'undo' or 'abandon' editing and recall the previously stored version of the document.

unjustified   Text which is not justified and which retains a ragged right margin.

updating files   Erasing any text no longer required prevents disks becoming cluttered with unwanted text and provides room for new text.

upgrade   Improvement of existing facilities, eg memory capacity.

upper case   All characters appear as capitals.

user defined key/keystroke memory   Some commands require a series of keystrokes in a specific sequence to perform a task. To assist the operator there may be a memory function allowing the sequence to be stored and recalled quickly and accurately when required. Keyboards with keys such as f1 f2 f3 often provide this facility.

user friendly   The system and/or program has been designed for the greatest ease and simplicity of use.

user manual   A company may prepare their own user manual to ensure there is standardisation of work presented to operators.

value added network (VAN)   In addition to basic transmission of data, subscribers may also have access to electronic mail facilities.

variable information   Part of a document which is subject to change, eg the name and address in a standard letter.

vertical scroll   The VDU displays a limited amount of text at any time, depending on the screen size, and to view additional lines in the document it is moved vertically up or down the screen.

video-conferencing   A teleconferencing facility offering verbal and visual facilities and possibly facsimile.

video display   An alternative name for the screen or VDU.

viewdata/videotext   Digital information transmitted via television signals (teletext) or telephone lines (Prestel).

Viewdata gives the public access to a large information database, using a television set as a terminal, existing communication lines, and very simple low-speed communications technology. The viewdata concept has been extended to private databases, still retaining the concept of inexpensive equipment and simple methods to provide quick and easy access to information.

Viewdata involves storing textual and graphical information in colour on a computer. Prestel was the first commercial viewdata service in the world. A viewdata-based bulletin display can replace the notice board, freeing the internal mail system from circulars, etc. For certain people the viewdata terminal will provide access to databases for specific trade or professional information held on external systems.

It is easy to use – simply press buttons on a key-pad as directed through the menus to the required information. Public systems are charged on a 'pay as you use' basis; the essential simplicity of operation keeps down the running costs of private viewdata.

visual display unit (VDU)   Displays text and operator information.

voice commands   Voice input is received via a microphone and digitised by an analog-to-digital converter so that the computer-based system can recognise and respond to it.

voice input A method of incorporating the spoken word with recorded text. The recipient of an electronic mail memo will note on his/her terminal that there is a voice message linked with a particular piece of text. An answer, eg 'I'll be able to attend the retirement lunch next week. Thanks.' could then be sent as a spoken reply.

voice output This is a relatively slow method of communicating information but there are obvious applications where sound is crucial, eg language translators, warnings or alarms. Great advances have been made recently in improving the quality and recognisability of machine-generated speech. A user-friendly terminal could speak instructions, error messages, and verbal verification of data being entered.

voice processing Input is via voice transmission rather than by keyboard, optical character recognition reader, etc.

voice recognition The computer matches the pattern of incoming signals from a microphone with stored 'templates' held in its electronic memory and thus recognises words and responds to a variety of instructions.

voice response An authorised user can dial into a suitably equipped computer system from any telephone and obtain verbal information.

voice synthesis The computer stores patterns of sounds to assemble words which can be played through a loudspeaker.

volatile memory A temporary memory where information is stored until the system is switched off.

wide document The average screen width for word processing is 80 characters which is adequate when using A4 portrait size paper (narrow edge at top). If a document is to be printed on A4 landscape (wider edge at top) then the complete document will not be visible on the screen as over 100 characters will need to be viewed and horizontal scrolling is necessary.

wideband A high capacity telecommunications channel.

widow line The first line of a paragraph which occurs at the bottom of a page.

Winchester disk   A powerful high speed, high capacity hard disk which is sealed in a special disk drive. Used with micros and mainframe computers where large storage capacity is important.

word/text processing   Typing, editing, storing, printing and communicating text with the aid of a computer. (See also **text/word processing.**)

word processing as a means of text production

Advantages

- Standard text is keyed-in once with less effort and then recalled on future occasions.
- Text being keyed-in can easily be corrected and the hard copy is error free.
- Text is keyed-in at high speed using special typing facilities, eg automatic carrier return, automatic centring, automatic underscore.
- Removes the need for repetitive typing, leaving the operator more time for less routine jobs.
- The operator can perform other tasks while the system is printing.
- Correction and proof reading time is reduced since only amendments require attention.
- Work is produced at high speed on a high quality printer.
- Text can be printed using special printing facilities, eg emboldening, justification.
- Personalised letters no longer have the appearance of being a standard letter with additions.
- 'Turnaround' time of documents is reduced, ie the document from original thought to final printed form is prepared more quickly.
- Pre-stored or default format settings save the operator time, eg margins, pitch, page length.

Disadvantages

- Operators may feel their work is repetitive and monotonous and that they work in isolation from others.
- Operators may have little opportunity to move away from the keyboard.
- Indecisive writers may be tempted to make many more revisions.

- Staff are sometimes reluctant to use the system.
- Time and effort required to learn how to use and maintain the system.
- Failure and breakdown of the system could result in a serious interruption to the workflow.
- System may be noisy and distracting for other staff.

word processing centre Word processing operators are grouped in one location, similar to that of a typing pool. The operators work as a team and a number of text authors use the services of the centre. In most cases it will be essential for the centre to be managed by a competent supervisor who will be responsible for overall control of staff and work of that centre.

Advantages

- staff and their work more easily controlled
- standardisation of work procedures
- even distribution of total workload between staff
- staff assessment and productivity easier to monitor
- specialisation of work by staff can be encouraged
- staff work as a team with others doing similar work
- training programmes easily undertaken
- economies in utilisation of floor space, equipment, heating, lighting.

Disadvantages

- control of large units sometimes difficult
- lack of personal contact between text authors and operators may lead to mistakes and misunderstandings
- personal identity of staff may be lost
- routine work may result in operators finding their work monotonous
- a centre may be ill-equipped to deal with confidential documentation
- a centre may be ill-equipped to implement proper security procedures
- machine breakdown can make a lot of staff idle
- in a large shared-logic set-up the operator may get very little job satisfaction and may never see the final printed work

- executives may find that they lose their personal secretaries and have to share one.

Typical examples of work undertaken by a Word Processing Centre:

Articles	Directories	Minutes
Catalogues	Form filling	Notices
Contracts	Handbooks	Price lists
Correspondence	Instruction manuals	Quotations
Customer records	Job descriptions	Reports

word processing secretary   A word processing secretary will transcribe on to the word processor via audio or shorthand dictation, enabling him/her to produce high quality accurate text quickly.

He/she must deal with organising the recording, housekeeping and security procedures involved when using a word processor and in addition should organise the use of the word processor for certain specific work, while using a typewriter for 'one off' tasks – essential when several secretaries share one word processor.

By providing a better secretarial service to the executives, they in turn are released from routine tasks and are then in a position to offer improved services to customers and clients.

word processing user   Text author who provides work for the word processing operator/secretary to undertake.

word processor   A word processor has many automatic functions operated through computer software which enable it to do much more than an automatic or memory typewriter.

All word processors can:

- file (write) documents to the storage medium
- retrieve (read) documents from the storage medium
- edit text – correct, insert, delete and repaginate
- centre, tabulate, re-adjust margins and columns, justify the right margin, paginate
- create personalised letters by merging two or more existing documents into one
- create documents by merging stored sentences, paragraphs, etc

- search documents for occurrences of particular words or phrases and change as necessary.

Exactly how much a word processor is capable of depends on the individual system, but many now also sort into alphabetical or numerical sequence, check spelling and perform simple arithmetic tasks.

Word processing is most cost-effective where standard text is required, eg letters, reports, legal documents, insurance policies, forms, updating information or price lists.

Word processors are a luxury for 'one-off' documents but, once an operator is experienced, the word processor is much preferred for all types of work because its automatic editing and correction facilities lead to much higher quality reproduction with less effort.

words per minute (wpm)   Describes either an operator's keying-in speed or the printing speed.

wordwrap/wraparound   The facility to carry a word to a new line if it will not fit in before the right-hand margin – note that a 'word' is regarded as any number of characters between one space and the next.

work-flow measurement   Productivity can be measured by counting the number of keystrokes per hour – this is not to turn operators into battery-hens but rather to assess the viability of the system. Keying-in speed is not the only measurement to be recorded. The real test of an efficient set-up is the turnaround time.

work procedures manual   An in-house manual should be prepared to enable operators and text authors to follow the company 'rules' regarding the processing of work via a word processing system. Both should be aware of:

– turnaround time	when required
– text corrections	standard correction symbols
– format/display instructions	margins, line spacing, page numbering
– draft/final copy	number of copies required
– printing instructions	single, one and a half, double
– special print instructions	emboldening, underscoring
– house style.	

work request form   To help the flow of work and minimise
misunderstandings a text author must complete a work request form
when submitting work, eg

WP WORK REQUEST FORM

Name: .... Date submitted: ....

Department: .... Date required: ....

DESCRIPTION OF WORK

New document .... Name of existing document ....

Original .... Draft .... Final .... Number of copies ....

Margins LH .... RH .... Ragged .... Justified ....

Line spacing 1 .... 1½ .... 2 .... As before ....

Paper – A4 Letterhead .... Plain A4 ....

Additional information/instructions

Disk storage instructions

Retain original .... Retain last version .... Delete from disk ....

Work undertaken by: ....

Date returned to text author: ....

work standards (quality control)   Acceptable standards of work
must be set and maintained with regard to accuracy of text typing,
text formatting, proof reading, housekeeping and security.
Increasingly, minor proof reading is left to the last draft stage, but
word processing's most outstanding benefit is the ease with which
text can be corrected. If an operator produces inaccurate work with
typographical and spelling errors, users will understandably have a
very poor opinion of the word processing facilities.

working disk   Contains files/documents of text created by the
operator.

working/internal memory Some of the memory will be *read only* and is stored permanently on a *read only memory* chip. Information stored on a *random access memory* chip will be lost when the system is turned off.

workstation A VDU, keyboard and printer make up a workstation. Several workstations may share a printer.

wraparound/wordwrap The facility to carry a word to a new line if it will not fit in before the right margin – note that a word is regarded as any number of characters between one space and the next.

write Text which has been keyed-in must be written to the storage medium to provide recall at another time.

write protect Disks can be protected by using the notch on the right-hand edge of the flexible disk. 8″ disks require this notch to be left uncovered but 5¼″ disks require the notch to be covered with the special write-protect labels supplied in each box of disks purchased.